Endorsements

"Why do we go to church? This simple answer: we've been invited. It's not our initiative but God's that brings us into the regular circle of his judgment and grace. He is the King and we are his people who have free access through the mediation of his Son. Exploring this amazing reality with solid biblical insight, this book offers a bracing, winsome and convincing adjustment in our approach. If all of our churches followed the wisdom here, the fruit would be enormous!"
—*Michael Horton, Ph.D.*
Westminster Seminary, California

"Guided by the Reformation principle of Sola Scriptura, Maldonado relentlessly pursues the truth that God is the author of His own worship. Although cognizant of the New Testament's primacy in shaping the public worship of the Church in keeping with the Gospel, Maldonado, to his credit, is not dismissive of the Old Testament—as if to regulate it almost to a 'non-essential status.' If one is looking for a primer on the corporate worship of the Christian Church, this book would be an excellent starting point."
—*Joe W. Kelley, Th.M., D.Min.*
Pastor and Seminary Professor, Emeritus
Providence Theological Seminary

"This is one of the finest and most encouraging books on worship I have read in a long time. The author opens up the true meaning and purpose of corporate worship in a way that will inspire and bless all who read it. In today's culture there are very few Christians who really understand the deep significance of biblical worship. This book will correct that problem. This is one book that I highly recommend for pastors and parishioners alike. When you read this book, the glory and wonder of true worship of the High King of heaven will open up before your very eyes. This is a book on worship that every Christian should have in their personal library."
—*Robert L. Dickie, Pastor Emeritus*
Berean Baptist Church, Grand Blanc, MI

"The holiness and majesty of God informs everything that Hexon Maldonado writes regarding corporate worship. God is actually present among His people when we gather together. We join in with the heavenly worship already taking place around His throne. Since God is the ultimate sovereign, he must not to be treated lightly, but approached with reverence. In fact, God himself reveals how we are to worship him. This book traces the theme of worship from the OT into the NT, showing how OT worship informs worship under the New Covenant. This is a concise biblical theology of worship that will ignite in your soul a desire to draw near to the very presence of God with the church."

—Allan Kenitz, Pastor
Reformed Baptist Church, Kalamazoo, MI

"Hexon Maldonado's wonderful new book unfolds the spiritual reality of corporate worship from the clear teachings of God's word. It is at the same time both theologically rich and accessibly practical. I highly recommend it to my fellow pastors and fellow believers alike. If taken to heart, the wisdom found within these pages is a gift which will deepen our weekly services by preparing and equipping the local church to gather together in reverence and awe into the very throne room of His Majesty the King for the purpose of glorifying and enjoying Him."

—Greg Van Court, Pastor
Dayspring Fellowship, Austin, TX

" This book is a solemn reminder for all that we serve a risen savior, who has called us into his presence not only to worship Him, but to witness His work and glory among us in a biblically prescribed way. Because what we do in worship shapes what we do in the world, following the lead of Pastors like Hexon Maldonado will help us recover the joy, blessing, honor, and reverence of entering into the King's presence in corporate worship."

—Rev. Jack Smith, Pastor Emeritus
Redeemer Presbyterian Church, Austin, TX

In the King's Presence

How Christ's Royal Majesty Enriches Corporate Worship (Revised)

Hexon J. Maldonado

In the King's Presence: How Christ's Royal Majesty Enriches Corporate Worship (Revised)
Copyright © 2023, 2025 Hexon J. Maldonado
Abounding Grace Publishing
All Rights Reserved.

Brief quotations from this resource may be used with conventional acknowledgments in presentations, articles, and books, and digital comparatives.

Unless otherwise indicated, all Scripture quotations are from The ESV Bible (The Holy Bible, English Standard Version®), copyright © 2001 by Crossway, a publishing ministry of Good News Publishers. Used by permission. All rights reserved.

ISBN: 979-8-218-67720-6

To my precious bride,

Terri Lynn

Acknowledgments

First and foremost, I would like to thank my God and King, Jesus Christ, for graciously and sovereignly granting me the incredible privilege, blessing, and honor of being given the right to be called a child of God, to come into his presence, to stand before his throne, to gaze upon his glory and to worship him. I am forever indebted to my King.

I would like to thank my precious wife for encouraging me to continue writing this book, even when the naysayers inside my head kept telling me otherwise. "He who finds a wife finds a good thing and obtains favor from the LORD" (Prov. 18:22). This is certainly true of you.

I would like to thank my dear friend and mentor, Dr. Joe Kelley, for carefully reading over the manuscript and providing me with invaluable feedback and advice. Throughout our many years of friendship, you have been a tremendous blessing in more ways than you realize. But I would also like to say thank you for allowing me to read your dissertation, "Seated in the Heavenlies: Integrating John Calvin's Principles of Worship in a Baptist Context" (2010). Your work had a tremendous impact on setting me on the right trajectory regarding worship.

Thank you to Robert L. Dickie for his book, *What the Bible Teaches about Worship* (2007), which helped me understand that what we do in corporate worship in the here and now should reflect how worship is taking place in heaven and how it will take place on the new earth. What we do on Sunday morning is practice for what we will do for all eternity. I also want to say thank you for taking the time to read my manuscript, providing me with invaluable feedback, and being willing to help a brother navigate the complicated and challenging world of publishing.

Thank you to Michael Horton for his wonderful work, *A Better Way: Rediscovering the Drama of Christ-Centered Worship* (2002), which reinforced in my mind that we ought to approach worship with reverence and awe. I also want to thank him for being so gracious and willing to read my manuscript and endorse it. But even beyond that, Dr. Horton has been a great influence on my life ever since hearing him speak for the first time at a Ligonier conference in Dallas in the late 1990's and then listening to him for years on his podcast, *The White Horse Inn*. I so appreciate his heart and his love for God's word and for God's people.

I would also like to thank those who have influenced me over the years and have helped to shape my thinking on this subject, though I do not personally know them.

I would like to begin by saying thank you to Greg Beale for his amazing and eye-opening lecture, "A Redemptive-Historical Perspective on the Temple" (2021), available at BiblicalTraining.org. His explanation of the meaning of the temple in the Old Testament and how it corresponds to the garden of Eden is outstanding. His lecture was significant in helping me tie all my theology of worship together and compel me to write this book.

A tremendous thank you to Peter J. Gentry and Stephen J. Wellum for their magnum opus, *Kingdom through Covenant: A Biblical-Theological Understanding of the Covenants* (2012). Their work gave me a grand panoramic view of what God is doing throughout redemptive history and helped me to better understand God as the King of all creation and of his Church. A special thanks to Dr. Gentry, my Old Testament and Hebrew professor, for having such a tremendous impact on this young seminary student simply by the way he carried himself and interreacted with his students. Dr. Gentry is one of the most knowledgeable and humble men I have ever met and will ever be a favorite seminary professor.

Though he is no longer here to read this, I must say thank you to the late Dr. R.C. Sproul for his excellent book, *How then Shall We Worship?: Biblical Principles to Guide Us Today* (2013). Dr. Sproul helped me see that the Old Testament still has much value and much to say about how we worship God in the New Testament church. Though we do not worship God in the exact same way they did in the Old Testament, many of those principles remain unchanged.

I would like to say thank you to my close friend, Bob Philips, who, years ago when I was in my mid-twenties, first helped me understand the importance of corporate worship and what is actually taking place in the gathering of the saints on the Lord's Day. I had intended to ask Bob to read and edit the manuscript for this book, but the Lord took him to receive his reward before it was complete. He is now fully experiencing what it means to worship in the presence of his King.

Lastly, but certainly not least, I want to thank my good friend and fellow church member, Shannon Johnson, for volunteering to painstakingly read over my manuscript, finding errors and smoothing out sentences and paragraphs. Your corrections and suggestions were invaluable. You are truly a good friend.

Contents

Foreword   1

Preface   4

Chapter 1: God as King   17

Chapter 2: Approaching the King   34

Chapter 3: The King's Throne Room   51

Chapter 4: The Role of Priests   67

Chapter 5: King Jesus   86

Chapter 6: Worshipping a Holy God   101

Chapter 7: Throne Room Decorum   116

Chapter 8: Inside the Throne Room   129

Chapter 9: Conclusion   149

Appendix A: Sample Liturgy for Corporate Worship   159

Appendix B: Confessional Readings for Corporate Worship   160

Appendix C: Scripture Readings for Corporate Worship   165

Works Cited   167

Foreword

This book on biblical worship was written by a man of God who grieves over the departure of the church from the biblical patterns of worship that have been taught in the Word of God. With great insight and passionate teaching, Pastor Hexon Maldonado leads us step by step into the holy of holies of biblical worship that takes place in the presence of the High King of heaven.

One of the most critical aspects of the life of every church is how that church worships God. I believe it can be said that the church in this 21st century is often irrelevant to the culture at large because its worship is so unbiblical and detached from the worship as taught in the scriptures. I have been preaching the gospel for over 50 years. It has been my joy to know Christian ministers from all over the world. I served on the board of Evangelical Press in Great Britain and worked with editors and authors with Evangelical Press, Banner of Truth, and other publishing companies. I have watched with great dismay how many churches, over the last 50 years, have gradually departed from the biblical patterns of worship. Hexon Maldonado has written a much-needed book on the subject of biblical worship. It is a joy for me to introduce to those who may read this book a minister who has a passionate desire for the church of Jesus Christ and a return to biblical worship. His heart beats for the glory of God. *In The King's Presence* captures the essence of what true worship is and where we've gone astray in the last number of years in our country regarding worship.

Pastor Maldonado understands that true worship must be more, much more, than just a desire to meet the felt needs of those who drop in on our services. True worship must bring us into the manifest presence of God and leave the worshipper with a sense of awe and wonder at that presence. Only when the church worships biblically will the church be a powerful weapon in the hands of God to bring lasting change to our culture.

I found this book to be helpful, challenging, and spiritually enriching to my faith. It created in me a desire to see my God as King! It fueled a desire for me to approach Him as the High King of Heaven. This book on worship will surely bless all those who read it with a desire to understand what true worship is about. We must take worship seriously because Jesus taught us that "true worshippers shall worship the Father in spirit and in truth: for the Father seeketh such to worship Him" (John 4:23). This is a book that is easy to read, extremely engaging, and very helpful on the topic of biblical worship.

I was immediately convinced by its contents that the author was a man who understood the actual issues confronting the church today regarding worship. I could feel his heartbeat on every page; I could sense the great burden he has for the church of Jesus Christ and the glory of God. In my opinion, reading this book on worship expressed the same concerns and burdens that many of the great preachers have had regarding worship. Many books can be purchased today on the subject of worship, and this book should be added to the list of must-read books on that subject. This book is written by a man who is passionate about his devotion to Jesus Christ and his desire to see the glory of God in the church.

When editing books for Evangelical Press in Great Britain, and deciding which books we should publish, I would ask myself, "Is this a book I would want my congregation to read?" "Is this a book that I would give to other pastors?" "Is this a book I believe has a practical message to help the church?" I believe

In the King's Presence is a book that meets those criteria that I've mentioned. One of the most encouraging and positive things anyone could say about another book when they've read it is this: "I've read this book. It blessed my heart. It added rich blessings to my life, and I would encourage others to read it as well!" That's how strongly I feel about this book by Pastor Hexon Maldonado. Open this book and begin your journey into the King's throne room. You will meet Him and worship Him!

—Robert L. Dickie
Senior Pastor, Emeritus
Berean Baptist Church

Preface

*You shall love the Lord your God with all your heart
and with all your soul and with all your mind.*
Matthew 22:37

    What is happening when we enter corporate worship, the gathering of the saints on Sunday? I don't mean, what things or events are going on? We all understand there is prayer and Bible reading and a sermon and worship music and singing. I mean, beyond the physical and visual and audio, what happens in corporate worship on a spiritual level, in a metaphysical dimension? Many Christians do not ever really ask this question. It doesn't seem to matter to them. What matters is that they enjoy what they see and hear and experience. What matters is that they get something out of it, that they are somehow blessed by it, benefited by it. Many Christians view corporate worship the way they view a grocery store. It's a good place to go, if they have what I want and meet my needs.
    The word *consumerism* has probably been over-used at this point, but it is true that much of evangelicalism has been plagued by a consumerist mentality. For many Christians, church has become about '*what I want*' and '*meeting my needs*,' rather than being about what God wants and pleasing Him. However, when churches begin catering to this consumerism, the result is that they begin to do what appeals to the masses. Church becomes more driven by business principles, rather than biblical principles, more driven by capitalism, rather than confessions, human greed, rather than God's glory.
    The problem, however, is much worse and runs much deeper. Churches being driven by consumerism are the product

of Christians having an over-inflated view of themselves—humanism cloaked in evangelicalism. Before there was consumerism, there developed a low view of corporate worship that began creeping into churches over a period of decades. It is no coincidence that consumerism began creeping into churches during the rise of the Industrial Revolution, late 18th century in Britain and late 19th century in the United States. The Industrial Revolution was driven by extreme competition for consumers which led to an explosion in private business and the rise of the first monopolies, immortalizing names like Rockefeller, Carnegie, and Vanderbilt. It was not long before churches began to take their cue from the corporate world and implement their principles into corporate worship. However, these principles never would have taken root had churches possessed a more biblical view of corporate worship. In the view of many evangelicals, the goal was to reach the masses rather than "guard the deposit entrusted" to the Church (1 Tim. 6:20).

The aim of this book is to help right the ship, to help churches get back on course, and to return to a view and understanding of corporate worship that will be glorifying and honoring to God. But in the end, does it really matter? So long as people are hearing the gospel and being saved, so long as people are on their way to heaven, does it really matter how we engage in corporate worship? Does God really care? Isn't all that matters is that we love God and that our hearts are in the right place, that our motives are pure?

The answer to all these questions is unequivocally 'yes!' However, what does it mean for our hearts to be in the right place, if not to love God with all our heart, mind, and strength? What God desires most from every believer is a heart that loves him supremely. When Jesus was asked which is the greatest commandment in the Bible, his response was to quote the *Shema*. "Hear, O Israel: The LORD our God, the LORD is one. You shall love the LORD your God with all your heart and with all your soul and with all your might" (Deut. 6:4-5; Matt. 22:37). What God desires above all from his people is love.

Some might argue that what God desires above all is faith. To be sure, justification is by faith alone in Christ alone and to God be the glory alone. However, a heart which loves God is a heart that trusts God, a heart which places faith in God. There is a reason Jesus did not answer the lawyer's question by citing some passage from the Old Testament (OT) which speaks about believing in God or placing one's faith in God. Yes, God wants us to have faith in him and in his word, to trust him, to obey him, to honor him, and glorify him. But all these are to be driven by a heart that loves him above all else—a heart which loves him supremely.

Thus, if we love God, if we appreciate what God has done for us, if we value Christ's death on the cross on our behalf, then our greatest desire should be to please and honor God in all that we do and speak. This would include the church; namely, corporate worship. Our love for God should drive us to believe that it really does matter what we do in corporate worship. It should drive us to scour the scriptures to see and understand all that God has commanded and prescribed to be done in corporate worship, rather than to take a flippant approach to worship, believing that faith is all that God cares about.

Our love for God and our appreciation for what he has done for us should compel us to want to live out the purpose for which we have been created and redeemed. The first question to the Westminster Catechism asks: "What is the chief and highest end of man?" The answer it gives is "to glorify God and enjoy him forever." This answer could not be better stated. In fact, all of creation exists to glorify God (Ps. 19:1; Rom. 1:20). Specifically, however, God calls and redeems a people to be his own so that they might bring him glory. In Isaiah 43:6-7, God says, "I will say to the north, Give up, and to the south, Do not withhold; bring my sons from afar and my daughters from the end of the earth, everyone who is called by my name, whom I created for my glory, whom I formed and made." God's people were created and redeemed to bring him glory. For this reason, scripture commands that "whether you eat or drink, or whatever you do, do all to the glory of God" (1 Cor. 10:31). To not strive to glorify God in all that we do, think, and say is to deny the purpose for which God created and redeemed us, the purpose for which Christ suffered and died.

What does it mean to glorify God? John Piper rightly states that to "'glorify [God] does not mean make glorious. It means [to] reflect or display as glorious."[1] We glorify God when we live, behave, speak, and worship in such a way that exults and magnifies God's awesomeness. We glorify God when we are driven by a passion to know and obey his word, even in the smallest detail, not from a sense of self-righteousness or Law-keeping, but from a heart filled with so much love for God there is an overwhelming desire to please him in everything, to give God our very best, knowing he is deserving of it and so much more.

The default position of evangelicals tends to be that we are saved by grace through faith and that God loves us just the way we are. While it is true that God loves his people despite our sinfulness, his unconditional love for us is the very thing which

---

[1] John Piper, *A Baptist Catechism* (revised), www.desiringgod.org.

should compel us to want to give God our very best and worship him in a way which brings him the most amount of glory. We must ever be mindful that although God's love for his people is unconditional and his faithfulness to his church is immutable, this does not mean it is not possible to grieve the heart of God and incur his discipline by our carelessness, disobedience, or flippancy (Eph. 4:30; Heb. 12:5-11). We would do well to remember the words God spoke to Moses when he did not do exactly as God had commanded him when he struck the rock at Meribah, rather than just speaking to it. "Because you did not believe in me, *to uphold me as holy in the eyes of the people* of Israel, therefore you shall not bring this assembly into the land that I have given them" (Num. 20:12, emphasis added). Moses failed to uphold God as holy in the eyes of the people, and he suffered the consequences for it. We cannot expect God to bless our churches when we fail to uphold him as holy in the eyes of the people during corporate worship, when we fail to uphold him as holy in the eyes of the people by the flippant and casual manner in which we approach God on Sunday morning, the way in which we enter the King's presence.

To be fair, there are many who argue that in order for the church to reach the lost with the gospel or to draw in the saints so they might learn and be equipped with God's word, the church needs to look and feel welcoming. Without realizing it, many churches have bought into the "seeker-sensitive" or "seeker-friendly" approach to corporate worship. Both these approaches are wrong-headed for at least two reasons. First, the primary purpose for the local church, the gathering of the saints for corporate worship, is not to reach the lost with the gospel. Communicating the gospel to the world, evangelism, is primarily (though not solely) the responsibility of the members of the church as they go out into the world for work, school, and leisure. This is what Jesus means when he says, "Go therefore and make disciples of all nations,..." (Matt. 28:19). The command in the Great Commission is not "*go*" but "*make*." The word *make* is in the imperative mood (the command form in the Greek). The word *go* is an aorist passive participle, which means it could be translated as "*While having gone*, therefore, make disciples..." In other words, the idea is that while Christians travel throughout the world, while they go about their business, they are to be about the business of making disciples.

To be clear, evangelism can and should take place at some point within the liturgy of corporate worship. We need to understand that on any given Sunday, there will likely be unbelievers seated among us, whether adult visitors or the children of members. For this reason, even the pastor who practices verse-by-verse expository preaching should, as Charles Spurgeon has said, "Start with the text and make a beeline for Christ." Ultimately, everything we do in corporate worship should point people to Christ as the only source of joy, satisfaction, forgiveness of sins, and eternal life. Nevertheless, the primary purpose of the local gathering of the saints for corporate worship is not evangelism, nor is it to feed the sheep. The primary purpose of the local gathering of the saints for corporate worship is just that—worship—*the worship of God*.

Within corporate worship, however, the saints do gather to encourage and admonish one another with "psalms and hymns and spiritual songs" (Eph. 5:19; Col. 3:16), to pray with and for one another (1 Tim. 2:1-2), to hear the reading and proclaiming of God's word (1 Tim. 4:13; 2 Tim. 4:1-2), to be equipped for the work of ministry (Eph. 4:11-12), and to partake in the sacraments (1 Cor. 11:17-34). Corporate worship is intended primarily for believers, not unbelievers.

A second reason the "seeker-sensitive" or "seeker-friendly" approach to corporate worship is wrongheaded is that the primary and only means of grace by which sinners are saved is the gospel. In Romans 1:16 Paul writes, "For I am not ashamed of the gospel, for it is the power of God for salvation to everyone who believes, to the Jew first and also to the Greek." Notice what Paul identifies as "the power of God for salvation," not the church, not corporate worship, not a seeker-sensitive, seeker-friendly, casual and laidback worship service, *but the gospel*. For this reason, Paul will go on to write that "faith comes from hearing, and hearing through the word of Christ"—*the gospel* (Rom. 10:17). How we conduct our worship services makes little difference regarding the salvation of sinners. Unregenerate, depraved, people will not be attracted to Christ because of what we do or not do in our worship services. Only the Holy Spirit working through the gospel has the power to open people's eyes to the glory of Christ and cause them to realize their need for a savior, and that Christ is that only and all-sufficient savior.

In fact, the seeker-sensitive, seeker-friendly, casual worship services prevalent in many evangelical churches has had the reverse effect and has made it more difficult for the church to reach the lost with the gospel. It is no coincidence that right around the same time the "seeker" movement was born, average church attendance in the United States began experiencing a steep decline. "The 'Seeker' movement was born in May 1974, when Bill Hybels and a team of close associates launched a new church in the Willow Creek Theatre located in one of Chicago's western suburbs."² This movement flowed into the Emergent Church Movement born in the last decade of the 20th century, which can be described as the "conviction that the influences of postmodernism on all Western societies demand that the church rethink and restructure its way of ministry lest it become completely marginalized and irrelevant."³ Yet, the very thing these two movements were seeking to avoid is the very end they helped bring about at a more rapid pace. According to a Gallup poll published in March 2021, "Americans' membership in houses of worship continued to decline last year, dropping below 50% for the first time in Gallup's eight-decade trend." Prior to 1975, church attendance among Americans held steady at around 73%. Beginning around 1975, church attendance began a gradual decline down to 47% in 2020.⁴ This is not surprising, because when the world looks inside the church and they do not see anything different from what is outside the church, then why bother? Why does church matter? When the world sees Christians treating corporate worship as ordinary and approaching corporate worship as less than the reverent and sacred event God intended it to be, why should we be surprised when the world (and often believers) are torn between attending church or going to the lake? If the gathering of the saints for corporate worship on the Lord's Day (Sunday) is not much different than sitting around, singing songs, and listening to a

---

² Joe Wayne Kelley, "Seated in the Heavenlies: Integrating John Calvin's Principles of Worship in a Baptist Context" (DMin. diss., Reformed Theological Seminary, 2010), 159.
³ Ibid., 133-134.
⁴ Jeffrey M. Jones, "U.S. Church Membership Falls Below Majority for First Time," Gallup, March 29, 2021, accessed December 29, 2021, https://news.gallup.com/poll/341963/church-membership-falls-below-majority-first-time.aspx .

Bible lesson, then what's the big deal? Can't these things be done in our own living room or while sitting on a lake in a fishing boat?

I would submit that having and practicing a high view of corporate worship is not a deterrent to the world or fellow believers, but an attraction. Having and practicing a high view of corporate worship causes unbelievers and believers alike to stop and take notice. It causes them to ask questions like: What is going on in there? Is someone important getting married? What is all the hoopla about? Why is corporate worship such a big deal to these Christians? I hope to answer these questions in the coming chapters.

Sadly, however, we too easily forget the immense price that was paid for the Church and the extreme value Christ places upon the Church—*his bride*. In Acts 20, as Paul is making his way to Jerusalem, he stops in Ephesus to give some final instructions to the elders of the church, not knowing if he will ever see them again. There he says, "Be on guard for yourselves and for all the flock, among which the Holy Spirit has made you overseers, to shepherd the church of God which He purchased with His own blood" (20:28, NASB). *Christ purchased the church with his own blood.* What an incredible bride-price he paid. Thus, we ought to approach church, we ought to take what we do in church, how we engage in corporate worship within the church, with great seriousness, reverence, and awe.

In describing what has happened to the church over the past several decades, Paul Washer states it well in the following illustration. This is a lengthy quote, but is worth citing in its entirety:

> Imagine there was a great king who loved his bride more than anything. And he's going to go on a long journey, and

before he goes on that journey he calls us, he calls you, he calls one man, and he says, "You will be the steward and you will take care of my bride. Now she's most precious to me. Here are the decrees by which you will care for her. This is what you shall do and shall not do with her. You must fulfill everything. Your faithfulness will be rewarded. Your unfaithfulness, your unconcern for these decrees regarding my bride will be punished." And so, the king goes on a long journey, and he's gone for a long time and the steward begins to notice that the people are losing interest in the king and they're losing interest in his bride, the queen, because she's somewhat pale and plain and old fashioned for them, so he decides that in order to save the kingdom he is going to remake the bride, and in doing that he's going to change her simple but elegant white robe into something a bit more eye-catching and flashy. He's going to paint her face and change her hair and then parade her in front of carnal men in order to attract them, somehow, back into the kingdom. When that king returns, what is he going to do to that steward? I'm sure he'll take his life. He'll judge him most severely. He'll look at him and say, "Who do you think that you are that you would do this to my bride, especially in light of the specific commands that I gave you?" And we can see the same thing today. We see so many men that are trying to transform, re-dress, re-package, the bride of Christ, so that worldly men might somehow be attracted to the King. I think those men should be extremely afraid.[5]

The Church is the bride of Christ, and she is so valuable to him that he was willing to step out of the glory of heaven and become

---

[5] *The Church Bible Study Set*, "The Church: Pillar and Ground of the Truth" (New Albany, MS: Mediagratiae, 2021), disc 1, timestamp 1:04:00.

human, to live the perfect life of obedience to the Law for her, and then to be beaten, flogged, and crucified on her behalf. In light of this truth, we ought to be extremely careful with how we handle Christ's bride, how we care for her. We ought to approach and enter corporate worship with extreme care and reverence. Within corporate worship we ought to be willing and desirous to offer God our very best.

The problem is not that Christians have too lofty a view of Christ and his Church, but they have too low of a view, albeit unwittingly. Many say they have a high regard for Christ and his Church but their behavior, how they conduct worship, what they do within corporate worship, says otherwise. I once read about a pastor riding his Harley-Davidson motorcycle down the aisle during worship service and up onto the stage just before preaching the sermon in order to provide a sermon illustration of some kind and nab his people's attention. I also once read about another pastor at a different church preaching his entire sermon while jumping on a trampoline. I myself once attended a church where the worship service seemed more like a rock concert than being in the presence of a holy God. During the singing portion of the worship service, the lights were turned off so that it was pitch dark, then a spotlight shone on the worship band, and the music was so loud I could feel it in my chest and could not even hear myself singing. And because I also could not see anyone else, or even my own hand, it seemed as though all the attention was being directed at the worship band.

In the end, what too many have lost sight of is that while it is true that Jesus is our friend and brother, before he was our friend and brother he existed from eternity past as God-Almighty (*El-Shaddai*), the Creator and sustainer of all that exist. This is the point John is making in the opening verses of his gospel. "In the beginning was the Word, and the Word was with God, and the Word was God." Jesus is God. Jesus has always been God. He then writes: "He was in the beginning with God. All things were made through him, and without him was not any thing made that was made." John wants his readers to understand that Jesus is the very same God of Genesis 1. Jesus is the God who spoke all things into existence by the power of his word. He simply *willed* creation into being. And it is this God, John says, who "became flesh and dwelt among us, and we have seen his glory" (1:14). Jesus is the great God and Judge and King of all the earth. And it is this view of Christ which should dictate how we approach and enter corporate worship, and what we do and don't do in corporate worship. It is this view of Christ that should compel us to scour the scriptures to see how God desires to be approached and worshiped. Not because we fear Christ and worry about what he might do to us, but because we love and adore him and desire to please and honor him in all that we do, particularly in how we engage in corporate worship.

Too many Christians are robbing themselves of experiencing the full blessing and joy of entering God's presence in corporate worship, entering the King's throne room. This is because too many possess an incorrect view of what corporate worship is, what is happening in the act of corporate worship. My hope and prayer is that this book will help right our course, will help return many churches and believers back to a biblical view of corporate worship, back to the joy, blessing, honor, and reverence of entering the King's presence.

At this point it must be noted that this book will not seek to answer all the questions regarding worship. Many stones will be left unturned. Throughout the last two millennia there have been many books, many wonderful and highly academic books, written on the topic of worship. This book does not seek to offer an exhaustive study of worship, rather this book seeks to get to the heart of worship. This book is about the meaning and spiritual reality of corporate worship. It's about what is happening in corporate worship on a spiritual level. It's about the heart attitude of those who engage in corporate worship. It's about how we should respond when we find ourselves standing in the presence of our King.

Chapter 1
God as King

Sing praises to God, sing praises! Sing praises to our King, sing praises! For God is the King of all the earth; sing praises with a psalm! God reigns over the nations; God sits on his holy throne.
Psalm 47:6-8

Most Americans tend to cringe at the idea of kingship or being under the authority of a monarch. In England, most understand the monarch to be more of a ceremonial figurehead, rather than an actual ruler with any actual authority. In their history, this stems back to AD 1215 when King John was forced to sign the Magna Carta guaranteeing certain freedoms to the British people. The reality was that the Magna Carta only guaranteed certain rights to the ruling class, and the Magna Carta was not always enforced. Nevertheless, this started England down the path toward a constitutional monarchy; that is, a monarchy whose powers are limited by the rule of law. Eventually, most of this was settled in England with the Glorious Revolution of 1688, which significantly reduced the power of the British monarch and granted the right for regular Parliaments, free elections, and freedom of speech in Parliament. Today, the British monarch is largely a figurehead, engaging in volunteer and humanitarian work. The Monarch does give an annual speech to Parliament, which is written by the government, and holds weekly meetings with the Prime Minister to grant council, which the Prime Minister can either follow or ignore. Apparently, however, the British crown "retains the right to claim ownership of any unmarked mute swan swimming in open waters…claims dominion over all whales, sturgeons and dolphins in the waters around England and Wales, doesn't need a passport to travel abroad, and can drive without a license."[6] Yet despite the British monarch's paltry authority, for many Brits the idea of England without a monarch is difficult to fathom. The monarchy is so ingrained in their culture and history that doing away with it is nearly unthinkable.

Americans in the United States simply cannot understand this way of thinking. When Americans think of 'monarch' within the context of U.S. history, what comes to mind is King George III, taxation without representation, the Boston Massacre, the Boston Tea Party, and the American Revolution. Americans believe that those who govern us should essentially be one of us. They should be elected from among us, should share our values and interests, and should be fully accountable to the people. To most Americans, the idea of bowing to anyone is loathsome and detestable. This makes sense in a Democratic-Republic born out of rebellion against the crown; however, the problem is that when Americans are brought into a saving relationship with Christ, we often bring into that relationship and into the church our Democratic-Republic views of government. We begin to read the Bible through the lens of *'we the people, by the people, and for the people.'* We tend to view our relationship with Christ much the same way we view our relationship to the President of the United States. *We elected him. We chose him. He governs by the consent of the governed. He is one of us.* This has had the effect of bringing Christ and his worship down to the lowest common denominator in many

---

[6] "What Powers Does Queen Elizabeth II Have?," *The Week*, December 10, 2019, accessed December 3, 2021, https://www.theweek.co.uk/royal-family/97645/how-much-power-does-the-royal-family-have

evangelical churches. For this reason, it is imperative that the concept of Christ as King be restored and proclaimed. Nevertheless, many Christians in the western world, particularly within nations void of the concept of monarchy, prefer to think of Christ as friend, brother, and shepherd. To be sure, each of these concepts regarding Christ are true and biblical. However, we cannot rightly nor accurately talk about God, including the gospel, without talking about God as King, or at least not without a sufficient understanding of his kingship. Throughout redemptive history, God accomplishes all his good pleasure with regards to his saving acts toward his people precisely because he is King. God is not King because of what he accomplishes. God accomplishes what he wills *because he is King*. The gospel—the life, death, and resurrection of Christ—can only fully make sense within the context of his divine kingship. Thus, fully knowing Christ and rightly worshipping Christ is only possible when we realize that before he became our friend, brother, and shepherd, he was and is the King of kings and the Lord of lords. Christ is not our friend who became King. He is *the King* who chose to become our friend.

God as the King of All Creation

From the very beginning of the Old Testament and then throughout the Old Testament, God is consistently portrayed as the King of all creation. The patriarchs, the nation of Israel, the prophets, and all the kings understood this. In their magnum opus, *Kingdom through Covenant*, Peter Gentry and Stephen Wellum state it well:

> Scripture begins with the declaration that God, as Creator and triune Lord, is the sovereign ruler and King of the universe. In this important sense, the entire universe is

God's kingdom since he is presently Lord and King. From the opening verses of Genesis, God is introduced and identified as the all-powerful Lord who created the universe by his word, while he himself is uncreated, independent, self-existent, self-sufficient, and in need of nothing outside himself (Ps. 50:12-14; 93:2; Acts 17:24-25). That is why the God of the Bible is the only true God, utterly unique, and unwilling to share his glory with any created thing (Isa. 42:8). This is also why God alone is to be worshipped, trusted, and obeyed; he is the King, and the entire universe is his kingdom.[7]

After Moses penned the book of Genesis, as it was given to him from God, what would have become clear to the Israelites from the opening chapters of the book is that God did not deliver them from Egypt simply because he is a more powerful God than the Egyptian gods, but because he is God of all gods. He is the one true God, the creator and sustainer of all that exists. This truth is echoed time and time again throughout the Pentateuch. As Abram is returning from rescuing his nephew Lot (Gen. 14), he comes across Melchizedek, king of Salem, whom we are told was "priest of God Most High." Melchizedek then blesses Abram and says to him, "Blessed be Abram by God Most High, Possessor of heaven and earth; and blessed be God Most High, who has delivered your enemies into your hand!" (vv.19-20). Thus, Abram is told and (by default) the nation of Israel is told, as they read Genesis for the first time, that the God of Abram is "God Most High" and the "Possessor of heaven and earth." He is the one who owns, sustains, and governs the universe. He is

---

[7] Peter J. Gentry and Stephen J. Wellum, *Kingdom through Covenants: A Biblical-Theological Understanding of the Covenants* (Wheaton, IL: Crossway, 2012), 592.

not simply the most powerful God. He is God of all gods. He is the King of all that exists, the sovereign ruler of all creation. This would have been made clear to the people of Israel as they read the account of Abraham in the book of Genesis for the first time, and it would have also been made clear in a dramatic display of awesome power as God brought down the ten plagues upon the land of Egypt and then destroyed the Egyptian army in the Red Sea. At the conclusion of this latter event, the people of Israel broke out in song and celebration in Exodus 15 and proclaimed, in part: "Pharaoh's chariots and his host he cast into the sea, and his chosen officers were sunk in the Red Sea. The floods covered them; they went down into the depths like a stone. Your right hand, O LORD, glorious in power, your right hand, O LORD, shatters the enemy" (vv.4-6). It was well understood that the Pharaoh of Egypt was thought to be a god, not just any god, but the most powerful god who ruled and governed everything. He was considered the Son of Ra, the sun god, and the incarnation of the god Horus. Thus, that the God who appeared to Moses in the burning bush was able to cast "Pharaoh's chariots and his host" into the sea was an awesome demonstration that he is the sovereign ruler of all.

The song in Exodus 15 then concludes with these words: "The LORD will reign forever and ever." The language of *reigning* is the language of kingship. The God of the Bible is not just a most powerful God. He is the King of creation. The difference between Israel understanding God as just a more powerful deity and understanding him to be the King of creation is significant. Many ancient pantheistic religions had powerful gods, but no one god completely ruled the others. There may be one who had more power than the others and, thereby, would exercise greater authority and influence over the others, but frequent battles would rage among the gods, and occasionally the lesser gods would gain the upper hand over the most powerful god or gods. Not so regarding the God of creation. The God who willed all things to exist, who destroyed all of creation with a flood, who entered a covenant relationship with Abraham, and delivered the Israelites out of Egyptian bondage, is "the LORD [who] will *reign* forever and ever."

The psalmist clearly understood this concept regarding the kingship of God. In Psalm 47:2 we read: "For the LORD, the Most High, is to be feared, *a great king over all the earth*" (emphasis added). Again, Psalm 95:3 says, "For the LORD is a great God, and a *great King above all gods*" (emphasis added). The idea of God as King is a refrain that runs throughout the Psalter (5:2; 44:4; 68:24; 84:3; 96:4; 97:9; 135:5; 145:3). The psalmists understood that God is not just a great God above many gods, but that he is the "great King over all the earth." He is not a president. He is not a prime minister. He is not a constitutional monarch. He is an absolute monarch. He is the sovereign ruler and King! He does what he wills to whom he wills when he wills, and answers to no one. The kingship of God was not something the Israelites simply extolled and sung about, but something that was actually witnessed at various points in her history. That is, there were times when God displayed his majesty to behold, or at least granted glimpses of it. In Isaiah chapter 6, about seven hundred years after the exodus, we read,

In the year that King Uzziah died I saw the Lord sitting upon a throne, high and lifted up; and the train of his robe filled the temple. Above him stood the seraphim. Each had six wings: with two he covered his face, and with two he covered his feet, and with two he flew. And one called to another and said: 'Holy, holy, holy is the LORD of hosts; the whole earth is full of his glory!' And the foundations of the thresholds shook at the voice of him who called, and the house was filled with smoke. And I said: 'Woe is me! For I am lost; for I am a man of unclean lips, and I dwell in the midst of a people of unclean lips; for my eyes have seen the King, the LORD of hosts!'

Notice that Isaiah sees the Lord "sitting upon a throne" and he sees the "train of his robe" *filling the temple*. In other words, God is so massive and so magnificent that Isaiah is only able to see the bottom half of a figure sitting upon a throne, and his robe, folded over on itself, fills the temple. The temple was a huge structure in Isaiah's day. The interior dimensions of the temple were ninety feet long by thirty feet wide by forty-five feet high. Yet, Isaiah says the "train of his robe filled the temple." We now understand why, when Isaiah sees the foundations of the threshold shake at the sound of the angels proclaiming "Holy, holy, holy is the LORD of hosts; the whole earth is full of his glory!", he cries out, "Woe is me! For I am lost; for I am a man of unclean lips, and I dwell in the midst of a people of unclean lips; *for my eyes have seen the King*, the LORD of hosts!" Isaiah finds himself standing in the presence of royalty, the King of all the earth, a holy and mighty God, and he recognizes his unworthiness to be in such a place.

Approximately two hundred years later, just before the destruction of the temple that Isaiah stood before, God would speak to Jeremiah the prophet and say to him,

But the LORD is the true God; he is the living God and the *everlasting King*. At his wrath the earth quakes, and the nations cannot endure his indignation. Thus shall you say to them: 'The gods who did not make the heavens and the earth shall perish from the earth and from under the heavens.' It is he who made the earth by his power, who established the world by his wisdom, and by his understanding stretched out the heavens. (10:10-12, emphasis added)

God says to Jeremiah that he is the "everlasting King." He is the king who has no beginning or end, whose reign endures forever, and he instructs Jeremiah that he is to say to the people of Israel and remind them that the false gods of the surrounding nations did not create anything. They are but carved statues (vv.3-5, 9) who cannot speak or act or create. Thus, God will destroy both them and those who worship them. The point, however, is that God is not king *because* he is able to destroy the false gods of the surrounding nations. God is able to destroy the false gods *because he is king*—the only king. He alone possesses sovereign power and might over all creation. One author rightly states,

> The image of YHWH as warring against the powers of chaos can be found in texts about creation, mount Zion, the Exodus, and the Day of the Lord. These texts show that God has become king in the act of creation and re-establishes his authority in history again and again by defeating the powers of chaos and evil until his ultimate victory on the last day. There has never been a time when God was not king.[8]

God as the King of Israel

One of the oldest concepts in the Old Testament with regards to the nation of Israel was that Yahweh was her king. While most of her surrounding nations viewed their earthly king as being the mediator between themselves and their god, Israel

---

[8] Jan Muis, "God Our King," *HTS Theological Studies* (2008), accessed December 3, 2021, https://www.academia.edu/50923215/God_our_King.

viewed themselves as being ruled directly by God himself.[9] This can be seen in several instances. For example, after Gideon defeats and kills the kings of Midian, Zebah, and Zalmunna, the men of Israel come to him and say, "Rule over us, you and your son and your grandson also, for you have saved us from the hand of Midian." Gideon responds to their request by saying, "I will not rule over you, and my son will not rule over you; the LORD will rule over you" (Jdg. 8:22-23). The people of Israel were looking for an earthly king, just like the surrounding nations had earthly kings, to rule over them but Gideon understood that God is not only the King of all creation, but he is also the rightful King of Israel. It is for this reason when they demanded that Samuel the prophet appoint for them a king like the surrounding nations, it was understood that they were rejecting God as their king.

> Then all the elders of Israel gathered together and came to Samuel at Ramah and said to him, 'Behold, you are old and your sons do not walk in your ways. Now appoint for us a king to judge us like all the nations.' But the thing displeased Samuel when they said, 'Give us a king to judge us.' And Samuel prayed to the LORD. And the LORD said to Samuel, 'Obey the voice of the people in all that they say to you, for they have not rejected you, but they have rejected me from being king over them.' (1 Sam. 8:4-7).

To be sure, God had always intended for the nation of Israel to have an earthly king. This is clear from passages as far back as Genesis 17, when God reaffirms the covenant made with Abraham in Genesis 15. There in 17:6 God says to Abraham, "I

---

[9] D.F. Payne, "King; Kingdom," in *The International Standard Bible Encyclopedia* (Grand Rapids, MI: William B. Eerdmans Publishing Company, 1986), 3:23.

will make you exceedingly fruitful, and I will make you into nations, and *kings shall come from you*" (emphasis added). This same promise is repeated to Jacob in Genesis 35:11. Now certainly if we trace the lines of both Isaac and Ishmael, we see that kings are found in the lines of both. However, God was not just predicting that there would be kings among his descendants, but that one day the nation of Israel will have an earthly king set over her. We know this from Deuteronomy 17:14-20, five hundred years before the time of King Saul, God gave Moses specific instructions and laws regarding the behavior of Israel's future kings.

The sin of Israel in demanding that Samuel appoint for them a king was due to the fact that in Deuteronomy 17:14-15 God specifically says to the people, "When you come to the land that the LORD your God is giving you, and you possess it and dwell in it and then say, 'I will set a king over me, like all the nations that are around me,' you may indeed set a king over you whom the LORD your God will choose." Notice the tail end of v.15: "*whom the LORD your God will choose.*" As we read the event that unfolds in 1 Samuel 8, God says to Samuel, "Obey the voice of the people in all that they say to you, for they have not rejected you, *but they have rejected me* from being king over them." By not waiting for God to choose an earthly king for them, they rejected God as their king. They rejected God as the King of Israel. They rejected God as having the authority to appoint Israel's king.

The Old Testament depicts God not just as the one Israel is to worship, but as the one who leads the nation of Israel. In Numbers 23:21-22 we read: "The LORD their God is with them, and the shout of a king is among them. God brings them out of Egypt and is for them like the horns of the wild ox." The imagery is of a king leading his people in victorious battle—"*the shout of a king is among them*" and "*God brings [leads] them out of Egypt.*" Unlike the gods of the surrounding nations, the God of Israel does not just sit above them, looking down upon them, waiting to be worshiped and appeased by his people. The God of Israel leads from the front and goes before his people into battle. Israel always understood that God was their king. He was not simply the one to be worshiped in Israel, he was the one who governs and rules over Israel. For this reason, the people often went to God in times of need, not as one who would go before a god in hopes of appeasing their god and securing his blessing, but as citizens who would go before their king believing the king has a moral duty to protect and provide for his citizens.

In Psalm 5:2 the psalmist prays, "Give attention to the sound of my cry, my King and my God, for to you do I pray." Again, in Psalm 44:4 the psalmist writes, "You are my King, O God; ordain salvation for Jacob!" That the people of Israel addressed God so often as *king* speaks to their understanding regarding the nature of their unique relationship to him. It was not just a vertical relationship, wherein the people worshiped and obeyed their king, but was also a horizontal relationship, wherein God their king would lead them in victory toward the promised land and toward their ultimate destination. The nation of Israel was keenly aware of this horizontal relationship with God. Unlike the gods of the surrounding nations, God is not despotic, but is leading them, caring for them, protecting them. He is at once an absolute monarch and a benevolent king. He is *their king* and shepherd.

That the nation of Israel viewed God as their king is seen in the fact that the temple was viewed as his throne room and the

Ark of the Covenant was understood to be his throne. In 1 Samuel 4:3-4 scripture says, "And when the people came to the camp, the elders of Israel said, 'Why has the LORD defeated us today before the Philistines? Let us bring the ark of the covenant of the LORD here from Shiloh, that it may come among us and save us from the power of our enemies.' So the people sent to Shiloh and brought from there the ark of the covenant of the LORD of hosts, who is enthroned on the cherubim." Regarding the Ark of the Covenant, we are told that God is "enthroned on the cherubim." The Ark of the Covenant was thought to be the very throne of God. So also, the psalmist proclaims in Psalm 99:1, "The LORD reigns; let the peoples tremble! He sits enthroned upon the cherubim; let the earth quake!" The God of creation "sits enthroned upon the cherubim." The implication becomes all too apparent when these texts are read in light of other passages, such as Psalm 68:24. "Your procession is seen, O God, the procession of my God, my King, into the sanctuary." If God is the King of Israel, and the Ark of the Covenant is the throne of God, and his procession leads into the sanctuary, then the temple atop Mt. Zion is the very throne room of God. God is their king. The temple is his throne room, and the Ark is his throne.

God Redeems People for a Kingdom

Though God is rightly king simply by means of being God and the creator and sustainer of all that exists, a king without subjects is like a general without an army, an admiral without a navy. Thus, from the very beginning, God always intended to redeem a people for himself to be brought into his kingdom. This is the reason given by God for delivering the people of Israel out of bondage in Exodus 19:4-6. There God says to

Moses that this is what he is to say to the people of Israel, "You yourselves have seen what I did to the Egyptians, and how I bore you on eagles' wings and brought you to myself. Now therefore, if you will indeed obey my voice and keep my covenant, you shall be my treasured possession among all peoples, for all the earth is mine; and you shall be to me a kingdom of priests and a holy nation.' These are the words that you shall speak to the people of Israel." Thus, God delivered Israel from Egyptian slavery in order to make them "a kingdom of priests and a holy nation." *His* kingdom and *his* nation. God did not deliver them simply that they might worship him and acknowledge him as God, but that he might be their rightful king and govern them, and they would be his loyal subjects, his kingdom. Understanding that sinful creatures easily forget the lessons and instructions of God, Moses reminds the people of this just before his death as he pronounced a blessing upon them.

This is the blessing with which Moses the man of God blessed the people of Israel before his death. He said, "The LORD came from Sinai and dawned from Seir upon us; he shone forth from Mount Paran; he came from the ten thousands of holy ones, with flaming fire at his right hand. Yes, he loved his people, all his holy ones were in his hand; so they followed in your steps, receiving direction from you, when Moses commanded us a law, as a possession for the assembly of Jacob. Thus the LORD became king in Jeshurun, when the heads of the people were gathered, all the tribes of Israel together. (Deut. 33:1-5)

"The LORD *became king* in Jeshurun, when the heads of the people were gathered, all the tribes of Israel together." God was not just a super-powerful, higher, spiritual being to whom they were to worship and be loyal. While all the nations of the world had a human king, who was often viewed as the son of their god and who would rule and govern the people, the God who delivered Israel out of Egyptian slavery was to be their king—their only king—who would rule and govern his people. This was a unique concept in human history—the idea that a nation would be ruled directly by God and not have a sitting human king. Nevertheless, Israel continued this way for the better part of five hundred years. God raised up prophets and judges as needed to guide and direct the people of Israel, always understanding that these prophets and judges were merely spokespersons for God, ambassadors as it were, who spoke on behalf of their one true king.

God was the king of Israel and Israel was his kingdom, not only by virtue of the fact that he is the creator and sustainer of all things or that he is the one who delivered Israel out of slavery, but by virtue of the fact that he would be the one to choose Israel's human king. As was previously stated, God always intended for Israel to have a human king, but when that time came, he would be the one to choose the king. "When you come to the land that the LORD your God is giving you, and you possess it and dwell in it and then say, 'I will set a king over me, like all the nations that are around me,' you may indeed set a king over you whom the LORD your God will choose" (Deut. 17:14-15). This is not dissimilar to the practice that existed in medieval Europe for several hundred years where the Pope, the head of the Catholic Church, would crown the incoming king. This lent to the idea that the king had been installed by divine appointment, but it also lent to the idea that the Pope, the head of the Church and representative of God on earth, was over the king. In this sense, God was telling the people of Israel that when they reached a point where they wanted or needed a human king, God himself would choose their king for them and appoint and install him. Thus, the human king of Israel was much like a puppet king. God himself was their true King. The idea of God as king meant that God had ultimate authority to rule and govern his people. God was not appointed by anyone. He has no royal lineage, no beginning or end. Thus, he is the sovereign, omnipotent, absolute monarch of Israel.

God as King Is to be Worshiped and Revered

Since God was rightly king over Israel and is the king of all creation, he is to be praised and worshiped for that reason alone. Certainly, he is to be praised and worshiped for all the many blessings he brings into our lives. But even if our lives are void of any discernible blessings, God is still to be praised and worshiped simply because of who he is, not just because of what he has done or will do for us. God is the King of the universe, the Creator and Sustainer of all that exists, and for that reason alone is to be worshiped and revered. The psalmist tells us in Psalm 47:6-8, "Sing praises to God, sing praises! Sing praises to our King, sing praises! For God is the King of all the earth; sing praises with a psalm! God reigns over the nations; God sits on his holy throne." The reason given that human beings are to sing praises to God and worship him is because "God is the King of all the earth." No other reason is given. No other reason needs to be given.

Later in Psalm 68:24-26, David extols, "Your procession is seen, O God, the procession of my God, my King, into the sanctuary—the singers in front, the musicians last, between them virgins playing tambourines: Bless God in the great congregation, the LORD, O you who are of Israel's fountain!" Here we are given the image of a great parade, a great procession, with God the King in the center, singers up front, musicians in the rear, and somewhere in the middle are virgins dancing and playing tambourines. And this procession, this "great congregation," is leading into the sanctuary, the throne room of our great God and King. This is an image and an event that took place not only in the Old Testament but, as we'll see later, takes place within the New Testament (NT) church, the corporate gathering of the saints for worship.

The idea that God is to be exalted and revered as King is so essential to Old Testament worship that the psalmist envisioned Jerusalem itself, the city of God, lifting her gates to worship and honor her King as he approaches the Temple, his throne room on earth. "Lift up your heads, O gates! And be lifted up, O ancient doors, that the King of glory may come in. Who is this King of glory? The LORD, strong and mighty, the LORD, mighty in battle! Lift up your heads, O gates! And lift them up, O ancient doors, that the King of glory may come in" (Ps. 24:7-9). The psalmist envisions the very gates of Jerusalem lifting themselves up, as if they were raising their hands in worship or in salute to their approaching God and King. This is the very same God the New Testament church worships today.

This is why sin and disobedience are such an affront to God. Gentry and Wellum rightly state that "Sin is essentially rebellion against the claims of the King—moral autonomy—and so, as a result of our sin, we now stand under God's judicial sentence of condemnation, guilt, and death (Gen. 2:16-17; Rom. 3:23; 6:23)."[10] The problem is that far too often present-day Christians want to detach the God of the Old Testament from the God of the New Testament, as though there is no continuity

---

[10] Gentry and Wellum, *Kingdom through Covenants*, 593.

between Old and New. On this point, R.C. Sproul insightfully states: "I do not know of anyone today who teaches pure, unvarnished Marcionism, but his heresy is alive and well in the evangelical church in our unprecedented neglect of the Old Testament. People, particularly in America, are conditioned to think of Christianity only in terms of the New Testament...Simply put, we have woefully neglected the Old Testament, just as if there is nothing but discontinuity between the two testaments."[11] While Sproul is talking about biblical worship and what that should look like within the context of New Testament worship, it is equally true that the people of Israel saw God as their King and, thus, approached and worshiped him accordingly. The people of God in our modern evangelical churches view him as their friend, their buddy, and pal, and approach and worship him accordingly. It is as though the God of the Old Testament and the God of the New Testament are completely different or that the God of the Old Testament ceased to be the King of the universe when he became incarnate.

---

[11] R.C. Sproul, *How Shall We then Worship: Biblical Principles to Guide Us Today* (Colorado Spring, CO: David C. Cook, 2013), 17. Marcion (84 - c.160 AD) taught that the God of the Old Testament was not the same God of the New Testament. He taught that the God of the OT was mean, vengeful, and vindictive, while the God of the New Testament (Jesus Christ) was loving, kind, and merciful. He was condemned by the Church as a heretic in AD 144.

Chapter 2
Approaching the King

Therefore let us be grateful for receiving a kingdom that cannot be shaken, and thus let us offer to God acceptable worship, with reverence and awe, for our God is a consuming fire.
Hebrews 12:28-29

One of the most well-known and loved hymns of all time is "Just as I am", written by Charlotte Elliott of Brighten, England (March 17, 1789-Sept. 22, 1871). The hymn was made even more popular by the late Billy Graham, as it was a favorite of his to be sung during the gospel invitation at his crusades. One of the most fascinating facts about this particular hymn is that, unlike many other hymns, we not only know who wrote the song, but we know when and where the song was written. We also know the circumstances surrounding the author's life and events which led her to compose this timeless classic. Around age 32, Elliott became an invalid. It is unclear why or how or what the debilitating illness or injury was, but we do know that it had a depressing and discouraging effect on her. She often battled with feelings of uselessness and insignificance. These feelings would come and go as she would battle back and forth between faith and despair.

Then in 1833, her father Charles Elliott passed away. He was a devoted Christian man and loving father whom she greatly admired. This only added to her melancholy and feelings of uselessness. Then one night in 1834, she lay in bed awake, turning over in her mind thoughts of being of little use to God because of her disability. She wrestled with wanting to do more for God but feeling helpless. When the morning came, she decided to put pen to paper as a way of encouraging herself and fighting away the dark clouds. The result was "Just as I am."

> Just as I am, without one plea,
> but that thy blood was shed for me,
> and that thou bidd'st me come to thee,
> O Lamb of God, I come, I come.
>
> Just as I am, and waiting not
> to rid my soul of one dark blot,
> to thee, whose blood can cleanse each spot,
> O Lamb of God, I come, I come.
>
> Just as I am, though tossed about
> with many a conflict, many a doubt,
> fightings and fears within, without,
> O Lamb of God, I come, I come.
>
> Just as I am, thou wilt receive,
> wilt welcome, pardon, cleanse, relieve;
> because Thy promise I believe,
> O Lamb of God, I come, I come.

The third stanza is telling and gives us insight into what she was struggling with that night when she penned this wonderful hymn. It is clear that when she penned the lines "just as I am…O Lamb of God, I come, I come" she was expressing her belief and faith in the biblical truth that God would accept her and redeem her and keep her in a covenantal relationship with himself despite her sins and flaws and physical disabilities. She was finding solace in the fact that "thy blood was shed for me…to rid my soul of one dark blot…whose blood can cleanse each spot." "Just as I am" is a song about God, the holy and righteous Creator, accepting man, the unholy and sinful creature, not because of anything we have done or can do—"without one plea"—but solely because of the life, death, and resurrection of Christ.

Yet, today many seem to think Elliott was writing about the idea that we can approach God in any manner we choose, that it does not matter how we approach God, how we come into his presence, or how we worship him. When we come to God, regardless of how we approach him, regardless of how we worship him, he is simply thankful that we have come. He doesn't really care how we come to him, just so long as we do. But is that really the case? Does God really not care how we come to him, how we approach him or how we worship him?

Abraham before God

In Genesis 17 God appears to Abraham and prescribes to him the sign of the covenant which was made between him and God back in Genesis 15. There in chapter 17 we read: "When Abram was ninety-nine years old the LORD appeared to Abram and said to him, 'I am God Almighty; walk before me, and be blameless, that I may make my covenant between me and you, and may multiply you greatly.' Then Abram fell on his face." What is worth noting is Abraham's response when he finds himself in God's presence. He falls on his face. Why does Abraham do this? Grant it, lying prostrate before a superior was the common practice of those living in ancient times. However, nowhere does God command people to lie prostrate before him in his presence.

Not only was lying prostrate before one's superior (and similarly, bowing) a common practice in the ancient eastern world but, in fact, it was common throughout all of Europe and (as far as we can tell) throughout the world. In fact, bowing was common practice in Colonial America and did not begin to be done away with until after the American Revolutionary War (1775-1781). This is because many early American leaders saw it as a vestige of British rule and believed that all Americans were equal (at least every American white landowner was equal). Nevertheless, elected leaders such as senators, U.S. representatives, and the President were all viewed as men with equal standing. Thus, bowing became a thing of the past and as democracy gradually began to spread around the globe, so also did the practice of not bowing to one's superior.

Abraham bowed before God because it was the common way of showing respect and reverence for a superior, and clearly God was and is his superior. Nevertheless, there was no requirement for Abraham to fall on his face before God. There was no societal law. There was no Old Testament commandment. God did not command him to do so. Abraham could have chosen to stand before God and greet him as a man would another man. He could have expressed to God that he respects him and has the utmost reverence for him, but that he simply does not see the need in demonstrating his respect and reverence for God by any external manner. He could have explained to God that while it is a common practice in his current culture to lie prostrate before a superior, the prevailing culture should have no bearing on how he expresses his respect and reverence for God. Furthermore, his unwillingness to practice the cultural form of showing respect and reverence should not be taken as any indication of his degree of respect and reverence for God. Besides, Abraham would have also known that God knows what is in his heart and mind. After witnessing all that God had done for Abraham thus far, after witnessing the fiery pot pass between the pieces of animals, (Gen. 15:12ff.), he would have known God could see in his heart and mind that he had a deep respect and reverence for him and left it at that. But he did not.

Abraham understood that words without actions are hollow. It is far more convincing, and therefore more reverential, to *show* his respect for God than to simply verbalize it. It was not enough for Abraham to simply possess reverence and devotion to God, it was not enough for Abraham to know that God knows this to be true and can see this in his heart, he wanted to *show* God his love and devotion and reverence. Thus, he falls on his face before God.

Moses and the Burning Bush

Fast-forward about five-hundred years and we come to Moses who is living in the deserts of Midian because he killed an Egyptian and is afraid for his life. The Israelites have been in slavery now for roughly four-hundred years (Gen 15:13; Acts 7:6) and so we read in Exodus 3, "And the angel of the LORD appeared to him in a flame of fire out of the midst of a bush. He looked, and behold, the bush was burning, yet it was not consumed. And Moses said, 'I will turn aside to see this great sight, why the bush is not burned.' When the LORD saw that he turned aside to see, God called to him out of the bush, 'Moses, Moses!' And he said, 'Here I am.' Then he said, 'Do not come near; take your sandals off your feet, for the place on which you are standing is holy ground'" (vv.2-5).

There was no particular reason, in and of itself, for the ground in that location to be holy. What made that particular patch of ground holy was that it was the designated meeting place with God. It was the place God had chosen to reveal himself to Moses. Certainly, God can be known through general revelation, but in the burning bush he reveals himself to Moses in a way like no other. Gentry states it well when he writes,

> In standing on the ground which belongs to God, Moses is not called *qādōš* [holy], but to be allowed to walk there he must submit to the practice of a rite or ritual: remove his sandals. Is this an innovation? Undoubtedly not. The act of removing one's sandals, like the act of the nearest relative in Deut 25:9 or Ruth 4:7, is a ceremony or rite of de-possession well-known in the culture of that time. The *gō'ēl*, i.e., nearest relative, removes his sandal to show that he is relinquishing his rights of purchase. Thus Moses must acknowledge that this ground belongs to God and enter into an attitude of consecration. Rather than marking an item as set apart, then, 'holy' ground is ground consecrated, devoted or prepared for the meeting of God and man.[12]

Thus, Moses removes his sandals to visibly acknowledge that the ground he is standing on belongs to God. Of course, God owns the entire planet, but he wants Moses to demonstrate he understands that God is the superior and Moses is the inferior, that Yahweh is King and Moses is his subject.

Gentry rightly notes that this was not an innovation by God. We see this being done not only in scripture (Deut. 25:9; Ruth 4:7) but there is historical evidence that this was the practice of the Egyptians when entering the presence of the Pharaoh, even

---

[12] Peter J. Gentry, "No One *Holy* Like the Lord," *Midwestern Journal of Theology* 12.1 (2013): 17-38.

if the Pharaoh himself was wearing sandals. It apparently communicated a sense of subservience and inferiority. Sandals could track dirt into the throne room. Sandals were also a means of comfort and some protection. Thus, to remove them is to display a measure of vulnerability. In short, when God commanded Moses to remove his sandals from his feet, Moses knew exactly the reason why. This was not novel. It would have made perfect sense in the mind of Moses.

What is worth noting, however, is that God demands that Moses comply with a cultural practice to *show* his submission and reverence for God. Certainly, God could have looked into Moses' mind and heart and seen that Moses understood himself to be subservient to God and that he held Yahweh in deep reverence and respect. Certainly, it was not necessary for Moses to remove his sandals from his feet in order to acknowledge the ground he is standing on belongs to God. Moses could have verbally acknowledged it, and God would have known he meant it. Apparently, it mattered to God that he externally demonstrates in some way his subservience to and reverence for God and for the ground he was standing on. It mattered to God that Moses externally and visually demonstrates he understands that being in the presence of God is extra-ordinary and should be treated as such.

The LORD upon Mount Sinai

In Exodus 19, God formally meets with the people of Israel from atop Mount Sinai. This scene is in preparation for the establishing of the covenant with Israel in chapters 20-24. Thus, in 19:9 God says to Moses, "Behold, I am coming to you in a thick cloud, that the people may hear when I speak with you, and may also believe you forever." We are then told that Moses communicated the words of the people to the Lord that they had spoken back in v.8, and then we read,

> the LORD said to Moses, "Go to the people and consecrate them today and tomorrow, and let them wash their garments and be ready for the third day. For on the third day the LORD will come down on Mount Sinai in the sight of all the people. And you shall set limits for the people all around, saying, 'Take care not to go up into the mountain or touch the edge of it. Whoever touches the mountain shall be put to death. No hand shall touch him, but he shall be stoned or shot; whether beast or man, he shall not live.' When the trumpet sounds a long blast, they shall come up to the mountain." So Moses went down from the mountain to the people and consecrated the people; and they washed their garments. And he said to the people, "Be ready for the third day; do not go near a woman." (Ex. 19:10-15)

The people are told to do three things in preparation for meeting with God—do not touch the foot of the mountain, wash their clothes, and abstain from sex. But should not God accept them *just as they are*? They have already professed to God that they will do all that he commands (v.8), so what is the point of these three requirements in preparation for meeting with God? Regarding this point, Walter Kaiser insightfully states,

> The theology of this passage, then, is fitness for meeting with God and preparation for the worship of God. What is required to approach the God of gods, King of kings, and Lord of lords is both *decorum* and a wholistic sanctification of our *bodies* as well as our inner persons. This is not to say that there was intrinsic virtue in the mere act of washing clothes or abstaining from marital relations, *but the outward*

41

act was to signal that the inner work of sanctification had also been sought.[13] (emphasis added)

In other words, it matters to God how we outwardly present ourselves when entering his presence, how we approach him, and how we prepare ourselves for meeting with him. Just as God required Moses to remove his sandals in order to acknowledge the ground he is standing on belongs to him, he goes a step further and forbids the people from stepping foot on the mountain in order to acknowledge the entire mountain belongs to him. God wanted the people to abstain from sex as a way of devoting themselves to God and not being distracted by the pleasures of the flesh. He wanted them to wash their clothes and present themselves appropriately for the King of kings and Lord of lords. He wanted them to don their best. Who would ever think to enter the presence of Pharaoh or any earthly king without his best and cleanest attire? So also, the people are to wash their clothes and look their best in preparation for meeting with their king. In other words, we may have a genuine love for God. We may have a deep reverence for God. We may be wholly devoted to God and to exalting him in worship, but God desires to see his people put forth the external effort of outwardly demonstrating our love, devotion, and reverence for him.

Strange Fire

In Leviticus 10 we read about one of the most tragic events in the Bible, a heartbreaking event wherein Aaron loses two of his sons in one horrible moment. There we read that "Nadab and Abihu, the sons of Aaron, each took his censer and put fire in it

---

[13] Walter C. Kaiser, Jr. "Exodus", vol. 2 of *The Expositor's Bible Commentary with the New International Version of the Holy Bible* (Grand Rapids, MI: Zondervan Pub. House, 1990), 418.

and laid incense on it and offered unauthorized fire before the LORD, which he had not commanded them. And fire came out from before the LORD and consumed them, and they died before the LORD." It is difficult to know exactly what Nadab and Abihu did wrong, but somehow they offered unauthorized fire before the LORD, fire which God had not commanded. Thus, it is important to note that we have no idea what their motives were. They may have been attempting to honor God. They may have been attempting to worship God. They may have been attempting to please God. Their motives may have been pure. None of that mattered.

For this reason, Moses says to Aaron, "It is what the LORD spoke, saying, 'By those who come near Me I will be treated as holy, and before all the people I will be honored.' So Aaron, therefore, kept silent" (Lev. 10:3 NASB). Regardless of what their motives were, they did not approach God in the way he had commanded and, thus, they did not regard God, they did not treat God as *holy* and they did not glorify or exalt God among the people. God is the king of his people, and what person in his right mind would approach their king in any way they desire? What sane person would disregard the manner in which their king has prescribed he be approached?

This passage loudly proclaims that God cannot and must not be approached willy-nilly, in any way we desire or deem to be acceptable, as if God should be thankful we are even willing to come into his presence. Aaron understood this, which is why he held his peace. This was a horribly tragic event for him, yet he says nothing because he knows Moses is correct. It would do no good to argue that their "heart was in the right place." It would do no good to argue that they meant well, that they were doing their best. God is the King of kings and Lord of lords and he expects to be treated as such and approached accordingly.

Fools Rush In

In 2 Samuel 6, we read about another tragic event regarding a man whose heart was definitely in the right place, whose intentions were pure. This is the story of David moving the ark of God to Jerusalem, the city of God. What should have been a joyful and festive event, turned into a tragic day. In fact, we are told at the beginning of chapter six that the day started out with great pomp and ceremony.

David again gathered all the chosen men of Israel, thirty thousand. And David arose and went with all the people who were with him from Baale-judah to bring up from there the ark of God, which is called by the name of the LORD of hosts who sits enthroned on the cherubim. And they carried the ark of God on a new cart and brought it out of the house of Abinadab, which was on the hill. And Uzzah and Ahio, the sons of Abinadab, were driving the new cart, with the ark of God, and Ahio went before the ark. And David and all the house of Israel were celebrating before the LORD, with songs and lyres and harps and tambourines and castanets and cymbals.

Picture the scene. David had gathered thirty thousand of his finest troops and all Israel, according to 1 Chronicles 13:5, and they are putting on this huge military parade with the ark of God leading the way. The ark was considered the very throne of God, the throne of Israel's king, "who sits enthroned above the cherubim" (1 Chron. 13:6). However, there are two tragic mistakes which are made. First, like all the kings of the surrounding nations, God had commanded that his throne be carried on the shoulders of four men, not placed on an ox cart (Ex. 25:14). What king would allow his throne to be placed on an ox cart and transported that way while he is sitting on it? Nevertheless, that is exactly what they do, and things do not go well.

The second grave mistake is recorded for us in 2 Samuel 6:6-7: "And when they came to the threshing floor of Nacon, Uzzah put out his hand to the ark of God and took hold of it, for the oxen stumbled. And the anger of the LORD was kindled against Uzzah, and God struck him down there because of his error, and he died there beside the ark of God" (vv.6-7). When the oxen stumbled and the ark began to slide off the cart, Uzzah reached out his hand to stop the ark from sliding off the cart and being damaged or broken. However, a second reason God had commanded the ark be carried with poles is because no one was ever allowed to touch the actual ark itself "lest they die" (Num 4:15). God is holy and all the furnishings inside the tabernacle/temple, inside the house of God, are holy and are to be treated as such. This means that nothing unholy should ever come in contact with the temple furnishings and, especially, the Ark of the Covenant. Nevertheless, Uzzah thought God would overlook his irreverent behavior because his motives were pure, his intentions were good. Uzzah would have done well to remember the words of the prophet Samuel to King Saul: "to obey is better than sacrifice, and to listen [is better] than the fat of rams" (1 Sam. 15:22). God our King desires obedience and to be treated and approached with reverence and fear. David and Uzzah treated the ark of God like household furniture. They did not treat it as *extraordinary* but as though it were *ordinary* and commonplace. Certainly, in his heart and mind, he knew it was special and thought of it as being special, but his external behavior said otherwise. Sadly, too often Christians do the same when entering the presence of the King during corporate worship. In their minds and hearts, they know this time is special and they think of it as being special, but the manner of their approach, their behavior, their appearance, and the way in which they worship says otherwise. The Bible makes clear that because Christ is King of his Church and King of all creation, he is not to be approached and worshiped in any way we think best simply because our hearts are in the right place and because our motives are pure.

The author of Hebrews exhorts his readers, "Therefore let us be grateful for receiving a kingdom that cannot be shaken, and thus let us offer to God acceptable worship, *with reverence and awe*, for our God is a consuming fire" (12:28-29, emphasis added). It should be noted that this passage is (1) a New Testament passage written to the New Testament church and (2) the reason the writer gives for worshipping God with "reverence and awe" is because "our God is a consuming fire." For some reason, New Testament believers have lost sight of God as a *consuming fire* and see him more as a cuddly teddy bear. They believe the God who struck down Uzzah was old and crotchety, but the God of the New Testament is soft and gentle.

O Worship the King

There is an interesting scene we read about in Matthew 2 when three magi traveled from the east to locate the infant Jesus in Bethlehem. There we read,

> And behold, the star that they had seen when it rose went before them until it came to rest over the place where the child was. When they saw the star, they rejoiced exceedingly with great joy. And going into the house, they

saw the child with Mary his mother, and they fell down and worshiped him. Then, opening their treasures, they offered him gifts, gold and frankincense and myrrh. (vv.9-11)
These were probably men from the region of Babylon who were well known for their scientific advancements, particularly in the area of astronomy. They also would have been somewhat famous for their supposed ability to interpret dreams and perform magic or sorcery. For this reason, *magi* would be the better term and not "wise men" since the underlying Greek word is *magos*. The phrase "wise men" comes from our older translations, such as the King James Version, mostly because in the year 1611 scholars were not sure what *magi* were.

Thus, these magi were Pagans. Why then were they following this star and why were they looking for the king of the Jews? During the Babylonian captivity, large numbers of Jews were exported to Babylon some 500 years before the birth of Christ. After the Babylonian captivity, when the Jews were allowed to return to the land of Israel, many of them stayed in Babylon. Thus, these well-read magi would have been familiar with the many stories that circulated throughout the entire region and the Old Testament prophecies about a Jewish messiah who would come from the line of David, from the tribe of Judah, and was to be born king of the Jews. The prophecy they almost certainly would have had in mind is Numbers 24:17. There Balaam prophesies over Israel and says, "I see him, but not now; I behold him, but not near: a star shall come out of Jacob, and a scepter shall rise out of Israel". They would have also been familiar with the promise God made to King David in 2 Samuel 7 to someday raise up an offspring from him who would establish his throne and his kingdom forever.

But why travel so far to worship this king if they are not even Jewish? And why did they first go to Jerusalem? In biblical times it was not uncommon for magi, nobility, and aristocrats to travel great distances to pay homage to the birth of a king in an effort to get in the king's good graces should he grow up to be a powerful ruler. Thus, in their mind it would have made sense that a ruler would be born in Jerusalem, the capital city of Israel. This explains why they came to King Herod and asked, "Where is he who has been born king of the Jews? For we saw his star when it rose and have come to worship him."

We are then told in v.11 that when the magi went "into the house, they saw the child with Mary his mother, and they fell down and worshiped him." They are not worshipping him as God because they don't know that Jesus is God or even the Son of God. They do, however, believe this infant child may be the next great political ruler of Israel. They believe he is the descendant of King David; the king of the Jews; the legitimate heir to the throne. This is apparent from the gifts they bring him, all very costly gifts. Gold, of course, makes sense. What better and more appropriate gift to bring a king than gold? Frankincense was an expensive incense used in religious worship but was also used by the wealthy to fragrance their homes. Myrrh was an expensive liquid perfume used to fragrance clothing, furniture, or to dip burial cloths in to diminish the stench of decaying flesh.

The point that cannot be missed is that these magi fall down and pay homage to this infant and bestow on him lavish gifts, not because they think Jesus will remember them, not because they are concerned about what others may think; they did not know anyone in Bethlehem and likely knew they would never see Joseph and Mary again, and not because it was expected of them. There were no expectations here. They bow before the infant Jesus and bestow very costly gifts upon him simply because they desired to *externally and visibly* display their reverence for the newborn king.

Humans are expressive creatures. In fact, we are the most expressive of all of God's creatures. There are certainly other creatures that are very expressive—cats, dogs, dolphins, apes, monkeys, etc. But humans are the most expressive. When humans are passionate about something, we sing. We compose music and poetry. We paint, sculpt, and create. We produce plays and musicals. And when we are invited to important events we get cleaned up, put on our best attire, and bring gifts, not because it's expected of us, but because we have a natural innate desire to outwardly express our inward thoughts and emotions. All humans throughout world history in every culture and every civilization have behaved this way. This is because we bear the image of our Creator. This is partly what it means to be created as the *image of God*. God is an expressive being and often chooses to express himself—to reveal himself—in ways that visually communicate to us certain attributes or aspects of his character.

In Exodus 3 God appears to Moses as a burning bush that "was not consumed." He could have appeared to Moses as a talking deer or just a voice from heaven. But a burning bush that was not being burned up communicates power, awe and wonder, light, and infiniteness. Fire is a source of immense power and life, and yet God's power is not diminished. The fire does not die down or burn out. When he appeared to the Israelites in the wilderness, he could have caused them to hear a soft and gentle voice from heaven but instead he appears to them with "thunders and lightnings and a thick cloud on the mountain" (Ex. 19:16), expressing power and might. God could have appeared to Isaiah as an aged sage but instead he saw "the Lord sitting upon a throne, high and lifted up; and the train of his robe filled the temple. Above him stood the seraphim. Each had six wings: with two he covered his face, and with two he covered his feet, and with two he flew. And one called to another and said: 'Holy, holy, holy is the LORD of hosts; the whole earth is full of his glory!' And the foundations of the thresholds shook at the voice of him who called, and the house was filled with smoke" (6:1-4).

God wanted Isaiah to know that he is the King of all kings and the Lord of all lords and that he desires to be worshiped and approached accordingly. Thus, the people of God respond in his presence in just such a manner. Abraham falls on his face. Moses willingly takes off his shoes. The Israelites gladly wash their clothes, and Isaiah proclaims "Woe is me! For I am lost; for I am a man of unclean lips, and I dwell in the midst of a people of unclean lips; for my eyes have seen the King, the LORD of hosts!" How then should we respond when we find ourselves in the presence of our King?

Chapter 3
The King's Throne Room

Therefore let us be grateful for receiving a kingdom that cannot be shaken, and thus let us offer to God acceptable worship, with reverence and awe, for our God is a consuming fire.
Hebrews 12:28-29

To properly understand the spiritual dimension of corporate worship, we need to develop a biblical understanding of Old Testament temple theology. This is because corporate worship is not an invention of New Testament believers. Corporate worship was not created *ex nihilo* (out of nothing), but rather is rooted in Old Testament temple theology and a biblical understanding of the person and work of Christ. To be clear, the pattern of New Testament corporate worship is not found in the Old Testament but was likely based to some degree on the gathering of Jews within the synagogue. Nevertheless, what is actually transpiring in the gathering of the saints for corporate worship is linked to Old Testament temple worship. However, to rightly understand Old Testament temple theology, we need to go all the way back to the garden of Eden.

The Garden of Eden as the Temple of God
The idea of the temple does not begin with the instructions God gives Moses in Exodus 25-30. Rather, the idea of the temple finds its origins in the garden of Eden.[14] Eden was the

---
[14] Greg Beale, "A Redemptive-Historical Perspective on the Temple," *Biblical Training*, accessed December 3, 2021, https://www.biblicaltraining.org/lecture/135848. This chapter has been greatly influenced by Beale's lecture; thus, I encourage the reader to listen

place where God met with his people, Adam and Eve, and dwelt among them. The temple in the Old Testament was the place where God would meet with his people and dwell in their midst (Ex. 25:8). The language God uses when he gives Adam instructions about what his role and responsibility are, language given to Adam not Eve, is the same language used with regards to the priests who were to minister within the temple. In Genesis 2:15, we read that the "LORD God took the man and put him in the garden of Eden to work (*abad*) it and keep (*shamar*) it." These two Hebrew words, *abad* and *shamar*, very often when used throughout the rest of the Old Testament are used with reference to the priests serving in the temple.[15] Thus, it would appear that Adam was to function as a kind of priest in the garden and was to work (*abad*) and keep/guard (*shamar*) the garden of Eden, and everything within the garden, much in the same way the temple priests were given the responsibility of working in the temple and guarding it.

This being the case, it is worth noting that this responsibility was not given to Eve, at least not directly. Adam is created and then placed in the garden and given the command to work and keep or protect the garden and not eat from the tree in the middle of the garden in 2:5-17, but Eve is not created until later (vv.21-22). The implication being that Adam was intended to protect and care for Eve as well and to minister God's word to her, the command which God had given him. Thus, Adam stands as a picture of the high priest in the Old Testament whose job it was

---

to it in its entirety. He does an excellent job of presenting OT temple theology. See also Gentry and Wellum, *Kingdom through Covenant*, "Connections Between the Garden in Eden and the Exodus Tabernacle," 213-216.
[15] Ibid.

to minister to God's people, and he stands as a picture of Christ, our great high priest, who ministers to the Church, his bride.

When Adam and Eve sinned, we are told that God "drove out the man, and at the east of the garden of Eden he placed the cherubim and a flaming sword that turned every way to guard the way to the tree of life" (Gen. 3:24). Thus, the entrance to the garden of Eden faced east. We then read that the entrance to the Old Testament temple faced east (Ex. 27:13). Additionally, Genesis 3:24 tells us that after God drove Adam and Eve from the garden "he placed the cherubim and a flaming sword that turned every way to guard the way to the tree of life." In Exodus 26, we are told that the veil which was to separate the Holy Place from the Holy of Holies was to "be made with cherubim skillfully worked into it" (v.31). So also, regarding the mercy seat, considered the very throne of God (Ex. 25:22; 2 Sam. 6:2), the people are commanded to "make two cherubim of gold; of hammered work shall you make them, on the two ends of the mercy seat. Make one cherub on the one end, and one cherub on the other end" (Ex. 25:18-19). Just as cherubim were placed at the east entrance of the garden to guard the way back into the presence of God, so also there were cherubim embroidered on the curtain as one entered from the east entrance into the Holy of Holies and there were cherubim placed on each side of the mercy seat (Ex. 26:1).[16]

Another indication that the temple was modeled on the garden of Eden, and thus the garden was the original temple on earth, is the images of plants and flowers which would have been seen inside the temple itself. For example, the lampstand which stood inside the Holy Place resembled a tree in its design.

---

[16] Ibid.

You shall make a lampstand of pure gold. The lampstand shall be made of hammered work: its base, its stem, its cups, its calyxes, and its flowers shall be of one piece with it. And there shall be six branches going out of its sides, three branches of the lampstand out of one side of it and three branches of the lampstand out of the other side of it; three cups made like almond blossoms, each with calyx and flower, on one branch, and three cups made like almond blossoms, each with calyx and flower, on the other branch— so for the six branches going out of the lampstand. And on the lampstand itself there shall be four cups made like almond blossoms, with their calyxes and flowers, and a calyx of one piece with it under each pair of the six branches going out from the lampstand. (Ex. 25:31-35)

We read in Genesis 2:9 that "the tree of life was in the midst of the garden." Then added to this, carved into the cedar walls inside the temple were images of gourds, palm trees, and open flowers (1 Kings 6:18, 29-35). The inside of the temple was designed to look like the garden of Eden. Like Eden, the Old Testament temple was the place where God dwelt in the midst of his people and met with them.[17]

The Purpose of the Temple

The temple in the Old Testament was intended to remind the people of God about what had been lost in the fall, but also to remind them that they had not been forgotten, that God had provided a way back into his presence, albeit limited. The temple reminded the people that God had remembered his covenant with Abraham that he would take them to be his people

---

[17] Ibid.

and he would be their God (Ex. 6:7-8). Of course, from the time of Moses, it would be another 1,500 years before access into the presence of God is fully opened for all his people through the life, death, and resurrection of Christ.

The temple was also designed to remind the people to keep their distance. Though God was now dwelling in the midst of his people, by means of the temple, only the high priest could enter into the Holy of Holies—the very presence of God—and that only once a year, and only after having offered a sacrifice for his own sins (Lev. 16; Heb. 5:3). Nevertheless, the temple was a reminder of God's grace and mercy and of his covenant fidelity.

Eden was the original dwelling place of God among his people. While God is omnipresent and exists in all places at once, in the garden God's presence with Adam and Eve was near and palpable. So also, in Exodus 25:8 God says to the people through Moses, "And let them make me a sanctuary, that I may dwell in their midst." God is omnipresent, and the people of Israel knew that, so it is not as though God needed a building in order to dwell among them and be present with them. But the temple was to serve as God's designated meeting place between himself and his people, or at least between himself and the representative of his people—the high priest. The temple was the designated dwelling place of God on earth. For this reason the temple is often called the "house of God." That phrase appears seventy-five times in the Old Testament with reference to the temple.

In this sense, the temple was intended by God to be his embassy on earth, a touch of heaven in the here and now. In Isaiah 66:1 God says, "Heaven is my throne, and the earth is my footstool; what is the house that you would build for me, and what is the place of my rest?" This text makes clear that heaven is the place of God's dwelling. Heaven is where God dwells, wherever that may be. Thus, heaven existed long before the earth, people, angels, stars, or the planets. Creation does not need to exist for heaven to exist. Heaven exists where God exists. And yet, we are told in Psalm 78:69 that God "built his sanctuary like the high heavens." The sanctuary on earth, the temple, was built and designed to model heaven itself (cf. Heb. 8:12; 9:23). Not that there are gourds and palm trees and blossoming flowers (though there may be), but that heaven is God's throne. Heaven is the *primary place* of God's dwelling. The temple was designed to function as God's embassy on earth. In other words, just like a foreign embassy inside another nation is considered—politically and legally—to be foreign soil and is not subject to the laws governing the nation within which the embassy resides, so also the temple was a piece of heaven on earth. It was the house of God—a celestial embassy in the midst of Israel.

Israel was established as a theocracy. For this reason, Moses and the Israelites, during their wilderness wandering years, never sought to establish a monarchy. Even under the leadership of Joshua, establishing a monarchy was never pursued. Certainly, Moses or Joshua could have made themselves kings had they sought to do so. They certainly had the charisma, the following, and the popularity. But they did not seek to make themselves king for the same reason Gideon gave to the people in Judges 8:23 when they tried to make him king for defeating the Midianites. "I will not rule over you, and my son will not rule over you; the LORD will rule over you."

It is not that Israel was never intended to have an earthly king. She certainly was. This is made clear from passages like

Deuteronomy 17:14-20. The mistake Israel made in appointing Saul as their first king was not waiting on God's timing and in desiring to have a king "like all the nations" (1 Sam. 8:4-9). Thus, God granted their request. He gave them a king *just like* the surrounding nations—one driven by greed, pride, arrogance, self-serving and self-protecting (1 Sam. 8:10-18).

Nevertheless, even after God established the rightful king upon the throne, the earthly king of Israel was always understood to be the servant of the Lord. God was the ultimate King of Israel. The human king upon the throne was God's servant to minister to the people on his behalf. This is indicated by the fact that the legitimate kings of Israel were always anointed by God's prophet; thus, indicating that God had set them on the throne and that their authority is derived from Him (1 Sam. 10, 16). The king of Israel was viewed as being God's anointed (1 Sam. 24:6; 26:9) and was viewed as being God's son (Ps. 2:7). The point, however, is that it was always understood that God himself was Israel's king (Ex. 15:2; Judg. 8:23; Ps. 93:1).

Understanding that God was Israel's king, and that the temple was the dwelling place of God on earth, a heavenly embassy, the temple was considered the throne room of God on earth, and the Ark of the Covenant was thought to be the very throne of God. The lid of the Ark was called the "mercy seat" (Ex. 25:17), and it was from the mercy seat that God communicated with the people of Israel and spoke to them. "There I will meet with you, and from above the mercy seat, from between the two cherubim that are on the ark of the testimony, I will speak with you about all that I will give you in commandment for the people of Israel" (Ex. 25:22). It is upon the mercy seat that God is enthroned (1 Sam. 4:4; 2 Sam. 6:2; 2

Kings 19:15; 1 Chron. 13:6; Isa. 37:16). The mercy seat, which sits above the Ark of the Covenant, was the very throne of God on earth. For this reason, no human was ever to lay a hand on it, and it was never to be transported by placing it on a wagon or cart (Ex. 25:13-14; 2 Sam. 6:6-7). No self-respecting king would ever allow someone to touch his throne or allow his throne, with the king seated on it, to be transported on the back of an oxcart.

That the temple was the dwelling place and throne room of God is further indicated by the attire of those who ministered in his presence were required to wear. In Exodus 28, God says to Moses, "Then bring near to you Aaron your brother, and his sons with him, from among the people of Israel, to serve me as priests—Aaron and Aaron's sons, Nadab and Abihu, Eleazar and Ithamar. And you shall make holy garments for Aaron your brother, *for glory and for beauty*" (vv.1-2, emphasis added). God intentionally wants those who serve in his presence as his priests to be dressed in a manner which reflects the one whom they serve—the King of Israel. Thus, they are to be adorned "*for glory and for beauty*." This is the common practice of every culture and the natural instinct of humans. No king, ancient or modern, would allow his servants into his presence in ragged attire and no one would dare enter the king's throne room in less than their best. Only the priesthood could enter the king's presence and worship him there and minister on behalf of God's people.

Thus, God instructs Moses to adorn the priests in splendid attire. As we read through Exodus 28, what becomes clear is that the material used to make the priest's garments was to be the very best. The symbolic nature of the design is understandable. For example, the two onyx stones which were placed on the high priest's shoulders, one on each shoulder, and were to have engraved on them the names of the twelve tribes of Israel, six on each stone, symbolized the idea that the priest was to bear the burdens of God's people. The twelve stones on the breastplate, each engraved with a name of one of the tribes of Israel, symbolized that the priest was to have affections for God's people and that they should be on his heart. But why must the names be carved into jewels and not into ordinary stones? Why must the ephod be made of "fine twined linen"? Why must the stones placed on the priest's shoulders be enclosed in "settings of gold filigree"? Why must the placard which reads "Holy to the LORD," which is fastened to the front of the priest's turban, be made of "pure gold"? God clearly intends that for those he calls to be his priests, for those called to enter his throne room and minister in the king's presence, he expects them to be adorned in accordance with the splendor and majesty of the one they serve. They are to be adorned for "glory and for beauty."

The Temple Points Forward to Christ

In John 2:18-22, after Jesus cleanses the temple, we read that a group of Jews asked Jesus, "What sign do you show us for doing these things?" Jesus answers them saying, "'Destroy this temple, and in three days I will raise it up.' The Jews then said, 'It has taken forty-six years to build this temple, and will you raise it up in three days?'" John then tells us that "he was speaking about the temple of his body. When therefore he was raised from the dead, his disciples remembered that he had said this, and they believed the Scripture and the word that Jesus had spoken." Jesus identifies his body as the temple of God and later New Testament writers take up this theological truth and flesh it out (Eph. 2:22; 1 Pet. 2:4-5).

The Old Testament temple was understood to be the dwelling place of God on earth. However, once we get to the New Testament, we are told that in Christ "all the fullness of God was pleased to dwell" (Col. 1:19; 2:9). While the temple was the designated dwelling place of God on earth, in the person of Christ, God takes on human flesh and dwells among us (John 1:14). Christ is not just the designated dwelling place of God. Christ is God dwelling with man.

Once we understand that the temple was the designated dwelling place of God on earth, we understand that the temple was the place where God's people could meet with him. In John 14:8-9 we are given the story of Philip essentially telling Jesus to quit beating around the bush and just show the disciples the Father plainly and they will believe. Jesus replies, "Have I been with you so long, and you still do not know me, Philip? Whoever has seen me has seen the Father. How can you say, 'Show us the Father'?" Anyone who has seen Jesus has seen God, has met with God, and spoken with God face to face.

The temple in the Old Testament was the place where God would speak to the people from above the mercy seat (Ex. 25:22). Yet the author of Hebrews tells us that "Long ago, at many times and in many ways, God spoke to our fathers by the prophets, but in these last days he has spoken to us by his Son, ..." (1:1-2). John tells us in "the beginning was the Word, and the Word was with God, and the Word was God" (1:1), and then tells us the "Word became flesh and dwelt among us, and we have seen his glory" (1:14). Whereas, in the Old Testament God spoke to the people from within the temple and from above the mercy seat, in the New Testament era God speaks directly to us through his Son who is the true temple of God.

In Ezekiel 40-47, the prophet is given a vision of a new temple. There are at least two interesting features about Ezekiel's temple. First, it measures a perfect square (41:13-14). The tabernacle described in Exodus, and also the temple which Solomon built, were rectangular. That Ezekiel's temple was a perfect square implies perfection, and likely points forward to Christ who is the true and perfect temple of God. That being the case, it explains why we do not see a temple on the new earth (Rev. 21:22). This is because Christ is the temple in whom we commune with God and fellowship with him.

A second element of Ezekiel's temple worth noting is that he sees in his vision an abundance of water flowing from underneath the threshold of the temple flowing east (47:1-6). In John 4:13-14, Jesus says to the woman at the well, "Everyone who drinks of this water will be thirsty again, but whoever drinks of the water that I will give him will never be thirsty again. The water that I will give him will become in him a spring of water welling up to eternal life." Then at the Feast of Booths Jesus says to the crowds, "If anyone thirsts, let him come to me and drink. Whoever believes in me, as the Scripture has said, 'Out of his heart will flow rivers of living water'" (John 7:37-38). Clearly what Jesus says to the woman at the well and what he says to the crowd at the Feast of Booths is referencing Isaiah 55:1, as well as Ezekiel 47. All who come to Christ in faith may drink in abundance of the living water which only he provides. Those in union with Christ, the true and perfect temple, by means of the Holy Spirit will have flowing from them streams of living water which, of course, ushers forth from the Holy Spirit himself. Fast-forward to Revelation 21:22 and there we read that Christ is the temple of God and that there is a river of life "flowing from the throne of God and of the Lamb" (22:1).

Thus, both the tabernacle and the temple in the Old Testament were designed to point us forward to Christ who is the true and perfect temple of God. For this reason, the temple was destroyed in AD 70, never to be rebuilt again.

The Temple Today

The Old Testament tabernacle/temple, leading up to and including Herod's Temple, destroyed in AD 70, were all designed and intended to be a picture pointing forward toward a greater reality—Christ. Now that the reality (*Christ*) has come there is no longer a need and will never be a need to bring back the picture (*the temple building*). Hence, there is no temple building on the new earth (Rev. 21:22). However, this does not mean there is no longer a physical temple for the people of God, that there is no longer a throne room on earth for God's people to enter and hear from him, that there is no longer a priesthood who minister in God's presence.

Writing to the church in Ephesus, the apostle Paul states: "So then you are no longer strangers and aliens, but you are fellow citizens with the saints and members of the household of God, built on the foundation of the apostles and prophets, Christ Jesus himself being the cornerstone, in whom the whole structure, *being joined together, grows into a holy temple in the Lord.* In him you also *are being built together into a dwelling place for God by the Spirit.* (Eph. 2:19-22, emphasis added). Paul makes clear that all believers are a "holy temple in the Lord" and that all believers together are "being built together into a dwelling place for God". This is not simply poetic or metaphorical language. Paul's theology and understanding of the Church was shaped and informed by his Damascus road experience. There in Acts 9, Paul is stopped on the road by the risen Christ who says to him, "Saul, Saul, why do you persecute me?" When Paul asks, "Who are you, Lord?" Jesus replies, "I am Jesus whom you are persecuting." Paul was persecuting and arresting Christians, yet Jesus asks, "Why do you persecute *me?*" From this Paul began to understand that all believers are the body of Christ as Christ indwells all believers (Gal. 2:20). He also came to understand that all believers are in union with Christ (Eph. 1:3-14). Thus, since Christ is the temple of God and Christ dwells in all believers and all believers are in union with Christ, then all believers comprise the temple of God. The temple of God continues to exist today. The temple of God is a *physical reality* since it is composed of *physical believers* who are in union with a resurrected and *physical Christ.*

In arguing that Christ is the second and greater Moses, the author of Hebrews points out that "Moses was faithful in all God's house as a servant, to testify to the things that were to be spoken later, but Christ is faithful over God's house as a son. *And we are his house*, if indeed we hold fast our confidence and our boasting in our hope" (Heb. 3:5-6, emphasis added). All believers are the house of God. God's house on earth, his dwelling place, did not cease to exist with the destruction of the temple in AD 70. The temple of God is just as real and physical today as it was when Solomon first built it. God's people are *real* and *physical*, and we truly are the dwelling place of God, the temple of the living God. The priests of God are also just as *real* and *physical* today as they were in the Old Testament era.

Peter understood this concept, for he writes, "As you come to him, a living stone rejected by men but in the sight of God chosen and precious, *you yourselves like living stones are being built up as a spiritual house*, to be a holy priesthood, to offer spiritual sacrifices acceptable to God through Jesus Christ" (1

Pet. 2:4-5, emphasis added). All believers are living stones being built into a spiritual house, a holy priesthood, to offer spiritual sacrifices. However, this is not to say that since all believers are the spiritual house of God, then there is no need for the corporate gathering of the saints on the Lord's Day because every believer is a church unto himself. On the contrary, the author of Hebrews commands us "to stir up one another to love and good works, not neglecting to meet together" (10:24-25). Gathering for corporate worship on the first day of the week is commanded by both prescriptive and descriptive texts (Acts 20:7; 1 Cor. 16:2; Heb. 10:24-25). The point being that just as in the Old Testament it was understood that God was omnipresent, but that the temple was the throne room of God and the designated meeting place between God and his people, so also the local corporate gathering of the saints on earth is the temple of God, the throne room of God, and the designated meeting place between God and his people. Within this temple, all believers are priests of God whose spiritual role and responsibility is to offer spiritual sacrifices to our God and King (1 Pet. 2:5, 9), sacrifices of praise, prayer, and worship. Thus, like God's priests in the Old Testament, when we enter the King's throne room, our appearance should reflect the One we serve and should be "for glory and for beauty" (Ex. 28:2, 40). Anyone who claims God is indifferent to how we dress when engaging in corporate worship and ministering in his presence have never carefully read Exodus 28 and 39. God expects his priests who minister and serve in his throne room, the corporate gathering of his people for worship, to adorn themselves in a manner which reflects the glory and the beauty of the One they serve.

This is not to say churches should require formal dress for people to attend church. We certainly must not return to the days when people were turned away from church because they were not properly dressed. The church must always be welcoming and loving to people of every race, gender, and economic class (James 2:1-7). Believers must never look down upon those who cannot afford more than what they are wearing or who have simply never been taught otherwise. However, it is to say that, within our ability, we ought to present ourselves in a manner which reflects the beauty and glory of God, the seriousness of the event, and the importance of the occasion. Christians tend to be better dressed for weddings, funerals, and retirement parties, than for corporate worship on the Lord's Day. The implication is that weddings, funerals, and retirement parties are important events—*church is not*. Church is academic, mundane, and routine. Church is a place where we learn, like a classroom or a conference. *But it is not the throne room of the living God.*

This sort of unspoken attitude is pervasive throughout many of our churches. To some degree this is a carryover from the Jesus Movement of the 1960's and 70's, which horribly mutated into the Emergent Church Movement of the early 2000's where skinny jeans, form-fitting t-shirts, and goatees were practically prerequisite for the clergy. Both these movements were an overreaction to the cold, traditional, and fundamentalist churches they saw around them. This younger generation of Christians viewed more traditional churches as being modern-day Pharisees, all polished on the outside, but dead and rotting on the inside. The response was to go in the opposite direction—to focus on pursuing holiness and godliness on the inside and not care about outward appearance. However, they threw the baby out with the bathwater. God is certainly *more concerned* about the condition of our soul (Matt. 23:25-28), but he also desires we treat him and approach him with reverence and awe. "Therefore let us be grateful for receiving a kingdom that cannot be shaken, and thus let us offer to God acceptable worship, *with reverence and awe*, for our God is a consuming fire" (Heb. 12:28-29, emphasis added).

How we dress for an occasion reflects the level of importance we ascribe to the event. When Christians treat the gathering of the saints for corporate worship as something less than serious and sacred, as something ordinary and mundane, we should not be surprised when the unbelieving world views church the same way.

It is a mistake to think that since the physical temple in Jerusalem was destroyed, since Christ is the temple, since all believers are in union with Christ, and Christ is in all believers, then the *Church* exists anywhere a believer is standing. The fullness of the Church does not indwell each believer. The fullness of the Church is *composed of all believers*. Each believer is a member of the Church, a living stone within the walls. Thus, the Church of God, the temple of God, the throne room of our King, is composed of all believers from every generation and throughout all ages but is most manifestly seen and experienced during the corporate gathering of the saints on earth in a single location. When believers gather for corporate worship, we come together as "living stones…being built up as a spiritual house" (1 Pet. 2:5). When believers come together for corporate worship, we reconstitute the temple of the God, enter his holy house as his priests, ministering in his presence and offering him the sacrifices of praise, worship, and adoration, and in that moment and in that place, the King speaks to his people through word and sacrament.

Chapter 4
The Role of Priests

But you are a chosen race, a royal priesthood, a holy nation, a people for his own possession, that you may proclaim the excellencies of him who called you out of darkness into his marvelous light.
1 Peter 2:9

Understanding that the temple is the throne room of God our King, and that the temple does not cease to exist with its destruction in AD 70, but rather that all of God's people comprise the temple, the question remains: where are the priests? Who are the priests? The existence of a temple implies a priesthood. A temple without priests is like an art gallery without art. Can it rightly be thought of as an art gallery, if there is no art? Would it not just be an empty building? For someone to point at a building and say, "That is an art gallery" implies there is art inside of it. If there is no art inside the building, then it makes more sense to say, "That was once an art gallery" or "that will be an art gallery." But without art, it is just a building—a cold empty shell.

Yet we are told in scripture that believers "are God's temple" and "like living stones are being built up as a spiritual house" (1 Cor. 3:16; 1 Pet. 2:5). Both preceding verses are in the present tense. The temple of God is not something that *once was* or something that *will be* but is a present reality. As we discussed in the previous chapter, all believers in union with Christ are the temple of the living God, the throne room of God, and that when believers come together for corporate worship, we reconstitute the temple of God. It may not look like Solomon's temple described in the Old Testament, but the temple of God was not always built from stone, timber, gold, and precious stones. Prior to the reign of King Solomon, the tabernacle, the mobile temple and throne room of God, was made from fabric, poles, and ropes. Thus, those who like to say "church" is not about the building, are correct. The Church, God's temple and throne room, is not comprised of brick and mortar and makes no difference if it is located in a living room, a theater or a gymnasium. Just as the temple was not about the material being used or the location but was about the presence of God and the designated meeting place between God and his people. So also, the temple of God does exist today. But who are the priests and what is their role?

Old Testament Priests

Before we can delve into this topic further, we need to at least have a cursory understanding of the priesthood in the Old Testament. This is not to say that what we see the priests doing in the Old Testament and the way we see them functioning is to be exactly modeled today in our churches. Clearly, there is much regarding the sacrificial system in the Old Testament that no longer applies today. Not because God simply went with a different way of doing things or a different way of saving sinners, but because much of the Old Testament sacrificial system finds its fulfillment, and therefore its completion, in the life, death, and resurrection of Christ (Gal. 3:24-29; Eph. 2:11-22; Heb. 7:12). Nevertheless, it is a mistake to think that since Christ has come, there is nothing in the Old Testament we can learn from and nothing that applies to the New Testament church. I once read an article years ago where the author states that "if it were not for U.S. laws, Christians would be free to marry their siblings since this is not forbidden in the New Testament." Obviously, such thinking is misplaced and dangerous. While this is not a book on hermeneutics or the proper place and application of the Old Testament on the New Testament church, suffice it to say that to argue that the coming of Christ means the abrogation of the entire Old Testament is overly simplistic. However, to argue that all the Old Testament is still binding is legalism. Rather, the Old Testament scriptures must be studied, understood, and interpreted through the lens of Christ—that is, through the person, teachings, and work of Christ. My Hebrew seminary professor would often say, "We cannot rightly understand the Old Testament until we first sit at the feet of Christ."

Identifying the Old Testament Priests

There is much to be learned from the Old Testament regarding corporate worship, the New Testament church, and the priesthood of believers. But first, who were the priests in the Old Testament? While the priesthood within the nation of Israel begins under the Mosaic law, the 'idea of priest' predates the Mosaic law as there were some persons prior to Moses who functioned as priests and some were even recognized as priests. For instance, previously we discussed the fact that the Garden of Eden was a sort of temple in that it was the designated meeting place on earth between God and man, and Adam was placed in the garden "to work [*abad*] and guard [*shamar*]" the garden and all it contained. This language is also used regarding Old Testament priests and their relation to the temple.

We also see that Job, who may have been a contemporary of Abraham, functioned as a type of priest for his family. In the first chapter of Job, we are told that his children enjoyed having frequent wild parties. Consequently, when the parties were over "Job would send and consecrate them, and he would rise early in the morning and offer burnt offerings according to the number of them all. For Job said, 'It may be that my children have sinned, and cursed God in their hearts.' Thus Job did continually" (v.5). Here we see the idea of the priest functioning as intermediary between God and man, seeking to appease the wrath of God toward those who have sinned against him in ignorance. The idea of someone mediating between God and sinful humans does not originate with the Mosaic law.

However, the first clearly identified priest in the Old Testament is Melchizedek who blesses Abraham after returning from rescuing his nephew Lot (Gen. 14:17-20). There we read that "Melchizedek king of Salem brought out bread and wine. (He was priest of God Most High.) And he blessed him and said, 'Blessed be Abram by God Most High, Possessor of heaven and earth; and blessed be God Most High, who has delivered your enemies into your hand!' And Abram gave him a tenth of everything." From this it appears that priests were viewed as being communicators of God, of being the ones to stand in the gap between God and man, and of being a means of grace to humanity. This is evident from the fact that, while Abraham apparently does not know Melchizedek nor has ever heard of him, he does not balk at receiving a blessing from him. Later, the author of Hebrews makes clear that this Melchizedek is a type of Christ who fulfills the office of priest, who has no beginning or end, and bestows *himself* as a blessing, not upon Abraham, but upon the offspring of Abraham (5:6, 10; 6:20; 7:1-19; cf. Gal 3:29).

In Genesis 41, after Joseph accurately interprets Pharaoh's dream, he elevates Joseph to the second highest position in the land of Egypt. "Only as regards the throne will" Pharaoh be greater than Joseph (v.40). In so doing, Pharaoh does five things for Joseph. First, he gives Joseph his own signet ring to wear on his hand. Second, he dresses him in fine linen and places a gold chain around his neck. Third, he allows him to ride in Pharaoh's second chariot, directly beside him. Fourth, he gives Joseph the new name of Zaphenath-paneah ("the god speaks and he lives"), indicating that Joseph speaks on behalf of God to the people (cf. v.38). And fifth, he gives the daughter of the priest of On to Joseph in marriage. That Pharaoh would place Joseph second in command and then connect him so closely to the Egyptian priesthood indicates the close association that was understood between authority and priesthood. Those who speak on behalf of God and who stand in the gap between God and humans by default possess and exercise a level of authority that is above ordinary humans.

In Exodus 3, we come to another individual functioning as a priest toward an important biblical figure. Right at the beginning of the chapter we read that "Moses was keeping the flock of his father-in-law, Jethro, the priest of Midian." It is worth noting how, prior to Moses, prominent figures in the Old Testament either functioned as priests in some way or were closely connected to priests (Adam, Job, Abraham). This is true of Moses as well, for we see in Exodus 18 that Jethro appears to be functioning as a priest on behalf of Moses, Aaron, and the elders of Israel. The Israelites had just come out of Egypt and Jethro hears about all that God had done for them and how he had delivered them from Egypt, and so he brings Moses' wife and two sons to him, who he had apparently left with Jethro to look after. But then we are told that after meeting with Moses, and after the initial greetings, Jethro "brought a burnt offering and sacrifices to God; and Aaron came with all the elders of Israel to eat bread with Moses' father-in-law before God" (v.12).

Later in the chapter, Jethro gives Moses advice on how to more efficiently govern the nation and then says to him, "'If you do this, God will direct you, you will be able to endure, and all this people also will go to their place in peace.' So Moses listened to the voice of his father-in-law and did all that he had said" (18:23-24). Thus, Jethro offers a sacrifice to God on behalf of Moses, Aaron, and the elders, and then gives Moses advice, which Moses follows.

The point is that the idea, function, and importance of priests are already in the mind of the Israelites as they come out of Egypt. It was understood that priests were the intermediaries between God and man. They spoke on behalf of God to the people, and they held a ruling/ministerial role within society. But who are to be the priests of God under Mosaic law? While the priests were to come from the tribe of Levi, not every Levite was a priest. Specifically, Aaron and his sons, and their sons, were to be the priests of God, with Aaron holding the position of high priest (Ex. 28:1; 29:9; 40:13). This is clearly due to Aaron being Moses' brother and assistant from the very beginning (Ex. 4:14-16). Thus, in the teaming up of Moses and Aaron we see the offices of prophet and priest working under the direction of God as King to lead and govern his people. All three offices would be fulfilled and carried out through the tri-fold offices of Christ—prophet, priest, and king.

The remaining Levites, on the other hand, were set aside to be the tribe from which the priests would come (the sons of Aaron), but by and large they were to function as assistants to the priests. This is evident from the fact that there is a consistent distinction between the priests and the Levites throughout the Old Testament (Ex. 28:1-5; Num. 8:14-19; 1 Kings 8:4; 1 Chron.

15:14; 23:2; Ezra 1:5).[18] Thus the Levites, who were not the direct descendants of Aaron and, therefore, did not function as priests, were given the task of assisting the priests. Their job was to minister to the priests, to keep guard over the temple and its furnishings, to guard the priesthood, and to transport the temple furnishings (Num. 3:5-10; 4; 18). Unlike the other twelve tribes, the Levites were not allotted land in Israel because they were chosen out of the world and out of the nation of Israel to be devoted to God and to have God as their portion and possession (Josh. 14:4). This seems to have been given to the Levites because of their zeal to do what is right in the eyes of God and their zeal for the Lord (Gen. 34:25; Ex. 32:26-29).

Thus, it appears that the Levites functioned as semi-priests or as assistants to the priests. They had access to the temple and were to transport the temple furnishings but could not come in contact with the temple furnishings. When moving the tabernacle, the priests had to first cover the temple furnishings and then the Levites would transport the items (Num. 4:1-15; viz. v.15). Nevertheless, in one sense all Israel was considered priests of God. In Exodus 19:6 God says to the nation of Israel, "and you shall be to me a kingdom of priests and a holy nation" and then says in Isaiah 42:6 that they are to be "a light for the nations." The idea is that just as the priests and the Levites were chosen out from the nation of Israel to serve God, to be devoted to him, and to stand in the gap between God and his people, so also the nation of Israel was chosen out of the world to serve God, to be devoted to him, and to stand in the gap between God and the world, to be a light to the nations and to point the nations back to God.

---

[18] The phrase "the priests and the Levites" appears twenty-eight times throughout the Old Testament.

The Role of Old Testament Priests

In discussing the role and function of Old Testament priests, the most obvious is that of being mediator between God and man. "For every high priest chosen from among men is appointed to act on behalf of men in relation to God, to offer gifts and sacrifices for sins" (Heb. 5:1). The giving of the Law under Moses made necessary the establishing of a sacrificing priesthood, which is why these two (the Law and priesthood) were given simultaneously. For once the Law of God had been given and the Mosaic covenant established, the Israelites stood condemned and guilty before God.[19] This is what the Law was designed to do (Rom 2:12; 7:7; Heb 10:3). The Law was never intended to save sinners or to cleanse their conscience. The Law cannot fix a person or put him back together. The Law can only tell a person he is broken and in desperate need of a Savior, someone to deliver him from the condemnation of the Law (Gal. 3:10; 5:3-4; Heb. 10:1-4). Thus, the priests were to act as a buffer between God and sinful man. They were to stand in *no-man's land*, as it were, the place where ordinary human feet dare not tread, and offer atoning sacrifices to appease the wrath of God and atone for the sins of the people (Lev. 1:3-17; 16:1-34). Only the priest could do this on behalf of the people because it was understood that the temple, especially the Most Holy Place, was the "realm of contact with God."[20] The temple was the designated dwelling place of God on earth among his people and only those who had been given the right and privilege of entering God's presence could do so (2 Kings 19:15; 1 Chron. 13:6).

---

[19] P.E. Hughes, "Priesthood," in *Evangelical Dictionary of Theology*, 2nd ed., (Grand Rapids, MI: Baker Book House Company, 2001), 952.
[20] W.O. McCready, "Priests and Levites," in vol. 3 of *International Standard Bible Encyclopedia*, 967.

This being the case, no physically blemished person could be a priest (Lev. 21:17-23), and no spiritually blemished priest could enter the temple (Lev. 16:1-14). Since God is holy and perfect in every way, those who minister in his presence must also be holy and perfect in every way. Not simply because they minister in the presence of God, but also because they represent God to the people. The priests minister on behalf of God as the mouth, hands, and feet of God to his people. Thus, their spiritual state and their physical appearance were to reflect the one whom they serve and the one on whose behalf they serve. For this reason, the high priest had to offer a sacrifice for his own sins before entering God's presence, and he was to be adorned "for glory and for beauty" in fine linen, gold, and jewels when entering the Holy Place (Ex. 28:2, 40). The symbolism of the priestly garments goes beyond the meaning of the breastplate or the robe or the turban which reads "Holy to the LORD" and has as much to do with both the material and the appearance of the apparel (Ex. 28:1-43).

The priests were also the ones primarily responsible for teaching God's laws to the people. When we think of those who spoke the word of God to the people and instructed the people concerning God's will in the Old Testament, we tend to think of the prophets. But before there were prophets (post-Moses), there was the priesthood whose job it was to teach the laws of God to his people. In fact, Deborah is the first person to be identified as a prophet in the Old Testament after the death of Moses (Judg. 4:4); however, she was not a prophet in the sense of speaking "Thus, says the LORD." The first prophet after Moses, who is like Moses, who speaks authoritatively on behalf of God is Samuel (a span of about 340 years later). Who then spoke the words of God to the people during that three-hundred-

and-forty-year interim between Moses and Samuel? —the priests. In Leviticus 10:11 God tells Aaron that his job as priest is "to teach the people of Israel all the statutes that the LORD has spoken to them by Moses." Thus, it was the job of Aaron and his sons, the priesthood, to ensure the people understood and followed the Laws of God.

Finally, another major role of the priesthood was to care for the temple, to transport the temple furnishings prior to Solomon's Temple, and to guard access to the temple (Num. 3-4). What is of particular interest, however, for our study is that the priests were charged with guarding access to the temple, thereby protecting the sanctity of the temple and protecting the people themselves. In Numbers 3:8-10 God speaks to Moses and commands that the priests "shall guard all the furnishings of the tent of meeting, and keep guard over the people of Israel as they minister at the tabernacle. And you shall give the Levites to Aaron and his sons; they are wholly given to him from among the people of Israel. And you shall appoint Aaron and his sons, and they shall guard their priesthood. But if any outsider comes near, he shall be put to death." Thus, the priests were to guard the "people of Israel", the "furnishings of the tent of meeting," which would include the tabernacle/temple itself, and against "any outsider" who comes near. Clearly the concern was not that God would be harmed by unholy persons entering the temple or touching its holy objects, but that any person who has not been granted the right to come near to God, to enter his presence, or to touch or handle the holy objects of his temple would face serious consequences. We will see later that the role and responsibilities of Old Testament priests continues into the present New Testament church.

The Destruction of the Temple in AD 70

In AD 70 the temple in Jerusalem was destroyed in fulfillment of Jesus' words (Matt. 24:2) and as punishment for all the "righteous blood shed on earth, from the blood of innocent Abel to the blood of Zechariah" (23:35). Jesus tells his audience all "these things will come upon this generation" and "your house is left to you desolate" (23:36, 38). The destruction of Jerusalem and the temple is one of the most horrific events to come upon the Jewish people, and certainly the worst to come upon any one city.

The Romans surrounded the city with an army of about 80,000 troops. They laid siege to it for five months beginning in April of AD 70. Because the siege began during the month of Passover, the Romans allowed the traveling pilgrims to enter the city for Passover but then refused to let them leave, thereby depleting the water and food resources of the city. After five months, many of them inside the city had starved to death. Any Jews who were caught outside the city or caught trying to escape were crucified and the crosses were set up on the surrounding hills across the valley all around the city, so as the Jews looked out over the wall from Jerusalem they would see Jews hanging on crosses everywhere. During the siege, the Romans built catapults all around the city that would launch 600-pound boulders into the city, crushing homes and killing people. Then as people died and mounting decaying bodies began to stack up inside the city, according to Josephus, the Jews threw over the wall as many as 100,000 bodies during the five-month siege. Finally, in August of that year, the Romans breached the walls of the city and slaughtered everyone inside. Caesar then ordered that the entire city be razed to the ground, and it was completely leveled. All that was left was a small part of the western wall, still there today, known as the "Wailing Wall." According to Josephus, when it was all over there were one million dead Jews inside the city of Jerusalem—one city! Over the next several weeks, as they hauled the bodies out of the city, Josephus reports that out of *one city gate*, they brought out 115,000 dead bodies.[21] Resulting from that horrific event, the Jewish people departed in all directions and scattered across Europe and would not dwell in their homeland again until the establishment of Israel in 1948. Since AD 70, the priesthood has come to an end...or has it?

The New High Priest

The temple of God still exists today. The temple of God exists and is reconstituted every time his people, the Church, gather for corporate worship on the Lord's Day. Thus, since there is still a temple, then it stands to reason there is still a high priest and a priesthood. But who are they? How do they function, and what is their role post-AD 70?

The Bible makes clear that Christ is the great high priest of his people. This point is spoken of and argued throughout the book of Hebrews. Right from the very beginning we read that Christ "had to be made like his brothers in every respect, so that he might become a merciful and faithful high priest in the service of God, to make propitiation for the sins of the people" (2:17). Thus, although the temple has been destroyed and the Aaronic line of priests forever lost, the people of God still have a high priest today who has entered the Most Holy Place, not with the blood of bulls and goats, but with his own blood, as of a lamb without spot or blemish, to make propitiation for the sins of his

---

[21] This paragraph has been adopted and modified from a sermon delivered by Hexon J. Maldonado titled "The End Times According to Jesus (Part II)" on March 21, 2020.

people (Heb. 9:11-14). Like the priests of the Old Testament, he stands in the gap ever interceding before the throne of God the Father on our behalf, on behalf of his people, for those who have placed saving faith in Christ (Rom. 8:34; Heb. 7:25).

Christ fulfills all the duties of the priesthood from the Old Testament. He stands in the gap between God and his people and mediates on our behalf, but we are also told from places like Leviticus 16:1-4 and 21:17-23 that the high priest, in fact all the priests, must be without any physical blemish and must be without sin, at least be without sin just before entering the temple. Of course, we are never given any description of Jesus' physical appearance, but it stands to reason that had he possessed some physical deformity or malady that would have been pointed out by the New Testament writers. Nevertheless, unlike the priests of the Old Testament, Jesus had no spiritual blemish whatsoever (*completely sinless*) and very likely had no physical deformity or malady. "God made him who knew no sin to be sin for us, so that we might become the righteousness of God in him" (2 Cor. 5:21).

The priests in the Old Testament were the ones responsible for teaching the word of God to the people. Of course, we are told in the opening verses of the gospel of John that Jesus not only came to make God's word known, but that he himself is *the Word*. "In the beginning was the Word, and the Word was with God, and the Word was God." We then read in v.14, "And the Word became flesh and dwelt among us,..." Jesus is the supreme revelation of God not only because he speaks the very words of God, but because *he is God*. The Old Testament priests spoke the words of God from the Law. Jesus is God in human form who came to earth to speak directly to the people without the medium of human priests or prophets.

The Old Testament priesthood was responsible for transporting and guarding the Tabernacle as they made their way across the wilderness to the promised land. Once Solomon's temple was built, their role then shifted to guarding the temple from those who would seek to violate it. Jesus himself, of course, is the temple of God (John 2:19-21). Thus, the temple is wherever Christ is. This is not to say that the temple of God is not on earth since Christ is seated at the right hand of God the Father (Acts 7:56), for we know that by faith and through the power of the Holy Spirit, all believers are in union with Christ and collectively comprise the body of Christ (Eph. 1:3-10; 2:19-22). Christ, being the temple himself, and all believers in union with Christ are the body of Christ, wherever the saints gather for corporate worship, whether it be in one location on one Sunday and then in a different location on the next Sunday, the temple of God moves with the body of Christ.

Christ is the one primarily responsible for guarding the New Testament temple (the Church) in that he says in John 10 that "he who enters by the door is the shepherd of the sheep. To him the gatekeeper opens. The sheep hear his voice, and he calls his own sheep by name and leads them out. When he has brought out all his own, he goes before them, and the sheep follow him, for they know his voice" (vv.2-4). Jesus is both the good shepherd who leads his sheep in and out of the gate, and he is also the one who guards access to the sheep, the Church, as the "gatekeeper." This is made clear from v.9 where he says, "I am the door. If anyone enters by me, he will be saved and will go in and out and find pasture." Jesus guards access to the sheep—the Church. And he is the good shepherd who will lay down his life to guard and protect the sheep (the Church, the NT temple), unlike the hired hands (vv.11-15). In every sense, Jesus fulfills the role and responsibilities of the temple high priest.

One question that often lingers, however, is how is Christ a legitimate high priest when the priests and the high priests were required to come from the line of Aaron and from the tribe of Levi? Jesus is a descendant of David, not Aaron, and is from the tribe of Judah, not Levi. The author of the book of Hebrews deals with this question honestly when he states,

> Now if perfection had been attainable through the Levitical priesthood (for under it the people received the law), what further need would there have been for another priest to arise after the order of Melchizedek, rather than one named after the order of Aaron?... For the one of whom these things are spoken [Jesus] belonged to another tribe, from which no one has ever served at the altar. For it is evident that our Lord was descended from Judah, and in connection with that tribe Moses said nothing about priests. (7:11, 13-14)

In other words, if the priesthood in the Old Testament was sufficient, then why did God raise up a second priest after the order of Melchizedek, who was not from the line of Aaron? He is honestly wrestling with an honest question. How can Jesus be our high priest if he is not a Levite?

The answer he gives is in two parts. First, he says in v.16 that Christ "has become a priest, not on the basis of a legal requirement concerning bodily descent, but by the power of an indestructible life." Christ has become a high priest by virtue of the fact that he is far greater and far above all human priests because he is from everlasting to everlasting. He has no beginning and no end. He is like Melchizedek who, at least within the context of the book of Genesis, appears to have no beginning and no end. He arrives on the scene, blesses

Abraham, and then vanishes. We don't know where he comes from or where he went.

The second reason he offers is that he was appointed by God. He says in v.21 (citing Ps. 110:4) that Christ "was made a priest with an oath by the one who said to him: 'The Lord has sworn and will not change his mind, "You are a priest forever."'" Thus, Christ is the new high priest for God's people, not because he is descended from Aaron but because God appointed him high priest.

The New Testament Priesthood

Since there is a New Testament temple and Jesus is the high priest of this temple, then there must be a priesthood. It is clear from the Old Testament that every priest must be a Levite but not every Levite was a priest. There was a distinction between the priests and the Levites (1 Kings 8:4). The priests were specifically responsible for ministering within the tabernacle/temple and for guarding it. The rest of the Levites were responsible for transporting the tabernacle. Nevertheless, all the Levites were a part of the priestly class and were responsible on some level for ministering to the broader nation of Israel. They assisted the priests, cared for and transported the tabernacle/temple, and interpreted the law of God for the people. For this reason, they were not given a portion of land as the other tribes were. God was to be their portion forever (Deut. 10:9; 18:2).

In the New Testament, we see this same idea carried forward into the Church. In 1 Peter 2:9 scripture says, "But you are a chosen race, a royal priesthood, a holy nation, a people for his own possession, that you may proclaim the excellencies of him who called you out of darkness into his marvelous light." All believers are a royal priesthood in the sense that we have all been set apart by God, appointed and ordained by God, to minister to the people of God and to be a light to the nations. Jesus tells us in Matthew 5:14 that believers are "the light of the world" (cf. Rev. 1:6; 5:10; 20:6). We are the priests of God whose job it is to be a light to the nations.

Furthermore, all believers have the responsibility of guarding the temple/church of God (Matt. 18:15-20; 1 Cor. 5:1-13; Gal. 6:1). All believers have the responsibility of teaching God's word to others, both inside and outside the church (Matt. 28:20; 1 Pet. 3:14-15). And all believers should recognize that this world is not our home (John 15:19). We do not belong here; therefore, we should not cling to this world and to the things of this world, recognizing that Christ is our portion and treasured possession (Ps. 16:5-6; Phil. 3:8).

All believers function in the same way as Old Testament priests. In the Old Testament only the priest had access to the very presence of God. Only the priests could enter the tabernacle/temple, which was considered the very throne room of God, the king of Israel. In Romans 5:2 Paul tells us that "through him we have also obtained access by faith", and then in Ephesians 2:18 he writes, "For through him we both have access in one Spirit to the Father." Of course, it is only because of Christ that believers are given access to the very presence of the living God. Nevertheless, as priests of God and because of the blood of Christ and imputed righteousness of Christ, we can "draw near to the throne of grace" (Heb. 4:16; 10:22).

Like the priests of the Old Testament, we draw near to God "to offer spiritual sacrifices acceptable to God through Jesus Christ" (1 Pet. 2:5). Those spiritual sacrifices include what we do on the Lord's Day in corporate worship, but are certainly not limited to that. Rather, the whole of our lives is to be offered up to God as a spiritual sacrifice and form of worship unto Him (Rom. 12:1-2). Just as the Levitical priesthood in the Old Testament were set apart and, thus, were to be wholly devoted to God, so also believers are to live lives which are wholly devoted to God. We are to pursue holiness without which no one will see the Lord (Heb. 12:14). To not strive for holiness and godliness in the Christian life is to fail to fulfill the priestly calling which God places on every believer's life.

This should not be taken to understand there is no difference within the church between the clergy and laity. Just as every priest had to be a Levite, but not every Levite a priest, so also every pastor/elder must be a believer, but not every believer is to be a pastor/elder. Just as there was a distinction between priests and Levites, so also there is a distinction within the church between those called to do the *ministering* and those who should be *ministered to* (Acts 11:30; 14:23; 15:2-6, 22-23; 17:20; 1 Tim. 3:1-7; 5:17, 19; Titus 1:5; James 5:14; 1 Pet. 5:1-5).

In all of this, it is important to note that the New Testament never speaks of priesthood in an individual sense but always in a corporate sense. For this reason, the New Testament never speaks of an "*office of priest*" but of the *priesthood of believers*. This is because without a temple there is no priesthood, and the corporate gathering of the saints is the temple of God. This is not to say that every believer is not a priest of God. He or she certainly is. Rather, it is to say that the priesthood is inextricably linked to the temple, and the temple exists when the people of God gather for corporate worship. The Aaronic priesthood came to an end once the temple was destroyed in AD 70 because the priesthood is meaningless without the existence of a temple. As each Levite wandered from the land of Israel, he might still think of himself as a priest but without a temple, there is no priesthood in any meaningful sense. So also, while every believer is a priest of God, the priesthood is most visibly seen and experienced when the temple of God is reconstructed by the saints gathering for corporate worship. Apart from the New Testament temple—corporate worship—there is no priesthood in any meaningful sense.

Chapter 5
King Jesus

*On his robe and on his thigh he has a name written,
King of kings and Lord of lords.*
Revelation 19:16

Winston Churchill once said, "The strongest argument against a democracy is a five-minute conversation with the average voter." In a democracy where the people elect their government officials, as time goes on, the government tends to look more and more like the people who elected them. This was one of the concerns of the founding fathers of the United States and one of the reasons they wrote into the Constitution the Electoral College to elect the President, which originally stated in the Constitution that "each State shall appoint...a number of Electors, equal to the whole number of Senators and Representatives to which the State may be entitled in the Congress" and that these Electors were to elect the next President of the United States. The Founding Fathers never intended for commoners to elect the President. Whether changing how the Electoral College functions is good or bad is not the point here. The point is that the Founders understood human nature. They understood that if average Americans were to directly elect the President of the United States, it would not be long before the President looked a lot like the average American. There may be a reason in the first 196 years of our nation's history that only one President faced impeachment, yet since 1973 there have been four Congressional impeachment trials.

As human beings, we tend to drag those in authority, and their respective institutions, down to our level because it makes us feel more comfortable. It makes us feel good about ourselves. When individuals or institutions who exercise authority over us present themselves in an elevated manner, it is viewed as insulting or condescending. It chafes at our pride. When I was an elementary student in a very large public school district (early 1980's), every male teacher wore a collared shirt, tie, and dress slacks, and every female teacher wore similar business casual attire. Today many public-school teachers wear jeans and polo shirts, and many school districts are encouraging teachers to allow students to address the teachers by their first name. I recall one Sunday, just a few weeks after starting a church-plant, we were meeting in the living room of a founding member, and I would wear a collared shirt and tie to deliver the message. After the service one Sunday morning, a gentleman who had been attending came to me and said, "Great message, pastor!" Then taking hold of my tie said, "Now if we could get you to lose the shirt and tie, we'd be doing even better!" Since that day there have been other hints over the years that maybe I should try being more casual. All the other "successful pastors" are sporting skinny jeans and t-shirts. Thus, democracy has found its way into our churches and pulpits. We want the guy behind the pulpit to look like my neighbor across the street. We want the worship team to look like the band at the nightclub. And we want our worship service to look like a rock concert—sanctuary pitch dark with a spotlight on the stage, and drinks and snacks served in the lobby that we can munch and sip on in the sanctuary while being entertained.

    The trouble is that Christians have lost sight of the holiness of God and the majesty of worship. In large part this is because

they have lost sight of the majesty of the *One they worship*. The late Dr. R.C. Sproul stated it well when he wrote,
> We are a people who have lost sight of the threshold and have begun to fail to make a transition on Sunday mornings from the secular to the sacred, from the common to the uncommon, from the profane to the holy. We continue, as did the sons of Aaron, Nadab and Abihu, to offer strange fire before the Lord (Lev. 10:1-2). We have made our worship services more secular than sacred, more common than uncommon, more profane than holy.[22]

Sproul is correct, and this is largely because many Christians fail to see Jesus as their King—*truly as their King.* Intellectually, they acknowledge that Jesus is King, that he is King of their lives, King of the Church, the King of kings and the Lord of lords, for these truths are undeniable from Scripture. Everywhere, we read that Christ is indeed King of the universe. *Practically*, however, many Christians do not acknowledge the kingship of Christ. They approach Him on Sunday morning in attire better fit for gardening than for an audience with their King. They approach Him during corporate worship with a heart attitude of indifference, at best, and legalistic requirement, at worst, rather than an attitude of great excitement, anticipation, and honor. They treat and approach with less reverence worshipping in the presence of the King of kings than they would having an audience with the President of the United States or the monarch of some great nation. Indeed, "We are a people who have lost sight of the threshold." All of this implies that either Christians do not view entering the King's presence as very significant or they do not truly believe they are entering the

---
[22] Sproul, *How Then Shall We Worship?*, 11.

King's presence. They do not believe King Jesus is truly present in that place. In the act of corporate worship, many believe they are there to learn about Christ, to worship Christ, and to pray to Christ. But Jesus is not *actually* in that place. We are not actually standing in the King's presence.

Some may question my reference to attire and see it as trivial or legalistic. To be sure, the Bible neither explicitly commands nor condemns certain attire in corporate worship. The concern here is not with *what is worn* in corporate worship, but *why it is worn*. It's about our perception of and attitude toward corporate worship. How one adorns oneself is always a reflection of one's perception of reality, whether they think something is real or not real, true or false. For instance, if you were sitting in your living room at home and your best friend walked in and told you that he just saw the Monarch of England sitting at a local coffee shop down the street and that the two of you should go see for yourselves because this is a once-in-a-lifetime opportunity, if you did go with your friend, you would likely go in whatever you were wearing because you would be doubtful that what your friend is saying is actually true. You might think it is just some joke or just someone dressed like the Monarch of England. However, if you and that same friend were touring England and he told you that he had secured passes to visit with the British Crown in Buckingham Palace and that you would be in attendance with other heads of states and diplomats and ambassadors, and he showed you the official passes to prove it, you would likely find your best attire to attend such an extraordinary event.

The difference between the first event and the second event is your perception of reality, of what is true and real. In the first example, you seriously doubted the *real* Monarch of England was *really* at a local coffee shop; thus, why not just go as you are? However, in the second example, you believed you were *really* going to Buckingham Palace to visit with the *real* British Crown in the presence of *real* heads of states and diplomats and ambassadors. To be fair, there are likely some who would go to visit the Monarch of England wearing shorts and t-shirt, and to do so would communicate one clear message—*this is an insignificant event*.

At best, many Christians doubt whether the gathering of the saints for corporate worship is *really* the throne room of the King and whether we are *really* standing in the presence of our King. At worst, many Christians *do believe* the gathering of the saints for corporate worship does become the throne room of our King and *we are standing* in the King's presence—*but this is an insignificant event*.

Christ Is King of Creation

The Bible makes clear that Jesus is the King of all creation. The apostle John clearly makes this point in the opening chapter of his gospel. "In the beginning was the Word, and the Word was with God, and the Word was God. He was in the beginning with God. All things were made through him, and without him was not any thing made that was made." These words are intentionally designed to echo the opening words of the creation narrative in Genesis 1. "In the beginning, God created the heavens and the earth. The earth was without form and void, and darkness was over the face of the deep. And the Spirit of God was hovering over the face of the waters. And God said, 'Let there be light,' and there was light." That Jesus is the very same God who created all things *ex nihilo* establishes that Jesus is the King of all creation.

John will continue to press this point throughout his gospel. By the end of chapter one, after Jesus tells Nathaniel he saw him sitting under the fig tree, he exclaims to Jesus, "Rabbi, you are the Son of God! You are the King of Israel!" (1:49). In chapter 6 we read that after Jesus fed the five thousand with five loaves and two fish, the crowd attempted to make Jesus their king by force (v.15) but he slipped through their midst because his time to ascend his throne had not yet come. Then at the beginning of his passion week, as he is riding into Jerusalem on a donkey, the crowd is waving palm branches and shouting, "Hosanna! Blessed is he who comes in the name of the Lord, even the King of Israel!" Then we read that "Jesus found a young donkey and sat on it, just as it is written, 'Fear not, daughter of Zion; behold, your king is coming, sitting on a donkey's colt!'" (12:13-15).[23] Throughout the gospel of John and, in fact, throughout all four gospels, Jesus is directly or indirectly called a king or *"the King"* thirty times. The idea is to drive home the point that Jesus is, in fact, a *real king*. He is not like many prima donna celebrities who like to think of themselves as a king, or even call themselves "the king". Jesus possesses real authority and real dominion and reigns over a real kingdom, and he continues to exist as a real person—*a real king*—seated at the right hand of God the Father (Eph. 1:20).

Christ's authority as king is not an ethereal authority but is a real, actual, and direct authority where he sustains, governs, and directs all creatures and events and sustains the universe by his

---

[23] That Jesus rides into Jerusalem on a donkey was not only to fulfill Zechariah 9:9 but was a common OT practice for a coronation ceremony to have a new king ride on a donkey or mule. These were not considered war animals; thus, for a king to ride in on such an animal was a symbol of peace and authority (cf. 1 Kings 1:38-40). David has Solomon, as the new king, ride in on his own mule.

power. It has already been established that the very same God who spoke the universe into existence is the same God who took on human flesh and became human. Thus, it can be said that Christ himself is the one who confronts Job and demands, "Where were you when I laid the foundation of the earth? Tell me, if you have understanding. Who determined its measurements—surely you know! Or who stretched the line upon it?...Have you entered the storehouses of the snow, or have you seen the storehouses of the hail, which I have reserved for the time of trouble, for the day of battle and war?" (38:4-5, 22-23). It is Christ who "makes nations great, and he destroys them; he enlarges nations, and leads them away" (12:23), who forms light and creates darkness, who makes well-being and creates calamity (Isa. 45:7), and who sustains the universe by the power of his word (Heb. 1:3).

This is not only because Jesus is fully God but because God the Father has chosen to "put all things under his feet and gave him as head over all things" (Eph. 1:22). God the Father has placed all things under Christ's authority and realm. To be sure, there will come a day when Christ gives all things back to the Father and will subject himself to the authority of God the Father (1 Cor. 15:24-28) but until that day, Christ reigns supreme from heaven and upon the earth. His kingdom is real. His power is absolute. His dominion is universal.

Christ is not only king with regards to his position and authority, but with regards to his role and responsibility. Christ carries out the function of a king in that he plunders the enemy's goods and gathers people to himself. In Matthew 12, after Jesus finishes exercising a demon possessed man, he is accused of casting out demons by the power of Beelzebul. In part, Jesus responds by saying, "if it is by the Spirit of God that I cast out demons, then the kingdom of God has come upon you. Or how can someone enter a strong man's house and plunder his goods, unless he first binds the strong man? Then indeed he may plunder his house" (vv.28-29). Jesus has come to conquer the enemy and to plunder his goods—people from east and west, north and south—and to gather a people to himself. Throughout much of world history, particularly during the Old Testament era, most of the world's population was under the power and control of Satan. However, once Jesus comes, Satan immediately begins losing territory and people as the gospel begins to go forward and Christ's kingdom begins advancing with it. Jesus has already previously stated that "many will come from east and west and recline at table with Abraham, Isaac, and Jacob in the kingdom of heaven, while the sons of the kingdom will be thrown into the outer darkness" (Matt. 8:11-12). As the gospel moves across the planet and people are regenerated by the sovereign power of the Holy Spirit, they are delivered from the domain of darkness and transferred into the kingdom of Christ (Col. 1:13).

Christ carries out the role of king in that once he establishes a kingdom of his own people, whom he has plundered from the enemy, he then gives them officers and laws to govern them. In the opening chapters of Matthew, the author clearly establishes Jesus as the second Moses, the second lawgiver. In fact, he establishes Jesus as one who is greater than Moses. Moses is called out of Egypt. Jesus is called out of Egypt (2:15). Moses passes through the Red Sea in a sort of baptism, along with the entire nation of Israel. Jesus passes through the Jordan River and is baptized (3:13-17). Moses wanders in the wilderness for forty years. Jesus wanders in the wilderness for forty days (4:1-11). Moses goes atop of Mt. Sinai and issues forth the Law which would govern the newly formed nation of Israel. Christ goes atop a mountain and begins to issue the laws which would govern the new covenant people of God (5:1-7:29), a people formed from every tongue, nation, and tribe (Gal. 3:28-29).

Christ, through his holy apostles, establishes officers within this new kingdom to teach and enforce the laws which govern his kingdom and kingdom people. In Acts 20, as Paul is making his way to Jerusalem, he stops in Ephesus and calls for the elders of the church and exhorts them to "pay careful attention to yourselves and to all the flock, in which the Holy Spirit has made you overseers, to care for the church of God, which he obtained with his own blood" (Acts 20:28). Elders are given the responsibility of being overseers for the church of Christ. Thus, in 1 Timothy 3:1ff. Paul offers explicit qualifications for those who desire the office of overseer. That elders/pastors are given by Christ to be the ones to care for and equip the church is made clear from Ephesians where we are told that Christ himself gave "the shepherds and teachers, to equip the saints for the work of ministry, for building up the body of Christ" (4:11-12). Just like any legitimate king, Christ establishes officers within his kingdom.

Christ supports and sustains his subjects within his kingdom. In Ephesians 5:29-30, drawing a point of comparison between Christ and his Church, and a husband and wife, scripture says, "For no one ever hated his own flesh, but nourishes and cherishes it, just as Christ does the church, because we are members of his body." It is Christ who nourishes the Church and provides all that she needs to survive and be healthy. In ancient times this is what all loyal subjects expected from their king, to somehow figure out how to ensure all their needs were met. And on some level, every king knew that if famine or pestilence or drought struck the land, he had to figure out a way to get food for the people or very soon he would not have a kingdom left. We see this happening in Genesis 41. "When all the land of Egypt was famished, the people cried to Pharaoh for bread. Pharaoh said to all the Egyptians, 'Go to Joseph. What he says to you, do.'" (v.55). When people are suffering, they will turn to their king and expect them to do something to solve the problem. Christ is the king who always ensures his people are cared for, protected, and sustained.

Finally, Christ functions as a king in that he restrains and conquers the enemies of his people. This is carried out both spiritually and physically. In Acts 12, after Peter had been arrested by King Herod, God sends an angel to rescue Peter from prison. So also, when Paul is in Corinth and is becoming frustrated by the Jews and Greeks being unwilling to listen to him (18:4), we read that God encourages him by opening the heart of Crispus, the ruler of the synagogue, so that he and his entire household believe and also many Corinthians along with him, and then telling Paul in a dream, "Do not be afraid, but go on speaking and do not be silent, for I am with you, and no one will attack you to harm you, for I have many in this city who are my people" (18:9-10). Apparently, Paul was so encouraged by this that he stays in Corinth for a year and six months (v.11).

Christ will not only restrain and conquer the physical enemies of God's people but also their spiritual foes as well. In Colossians we are told that God the Father "has delivered us from the domain of darkness and transferred us to the kingdom of his beloved Son" (1:13). If the kingdom we are in belongs to Christ, then Christ is the king of this kingdom. We are then told that this is accomplished and takes place through the work and death of Christ, for it is he who canceled "the record of debt that stood against us with its legal demands. This he set aside, nailing it to the cross. He disarmed the rulers and authorities and put them to open shame, by triumphing over them in him" (Col. 2:14-15). Christ disarmed the rulers and authorities and put them to open shame by triumphing over them through his life, death, and resurrection. This is battlefield language being used. Christ is the triumphant and victorious king who rescues and delivers his people out of spiritual bondage. He frees them from the shackles which bind them and brings them under his domain and protection and authority.

Throughout scripture, Christ carries out the role and functions of a king by calling a people to himself, giving his people officers and laws to govern them, supporting and sustaining them, and restraining and conquering their enemies.

Christ Is King Over His Church

The Bible speaks of Christ as being the coming king. This truth is spoken of and prophesied in the Old Testament and then recognized as coming to fruition in the New Testament. The psalmist sings to God and writes: "You ascended on high, leading a host of captives in your train and receiving gifts among men, even among the rebellious, that the LORD God may dwell there" (68:18). Paul cites this passage when speaking about Christ and all that he does for the church (Eph 4:8). What cannot be overlooked, however, is that the language of ascending on high and leading a host of captives is regal/battlefield language designed to point the reader towards the kingship of Christ.

The Puritans, and especially [Edward] Reynolds, addressed the issue of Christ's exaltation in relation to His kingship. The exaltation of Christ as king is fully realized at His enthronement. But at His ascension, according to [Thomas]

Goodwin, a military triumph is accorded Him ("leading captivity captive" [Ps. 68:18; Eph. 4:8]), which shows that He did in fact subdue His enemies at the cross. The enthronement of Christ, however, is the full realization of His triumph over His enemies and has royal power to bless the church with the promised Holy Spirit.[24]

The ascension and enthronement of Christ demonstrates that Christ not only triumphed over his enemies and the enemies of his people, but that he is the head of the church and of his kingdom. He is the king upon his throne and is ruling upon the earth. Thus, for instance, we read in Ephesians 1:22 that God the Father "put all things under his feet and gave him as head over all things to the church,..." Everything in the church, in the world, in the universe, has been placed under the feet of Christ, under his authority. The idea of being placed under his feet conjures up images of a king's royal footstool. Christ is the head of the church. He is the king in every sense of the word (Eph. 5:23).

Given that Christ is a king, then where is his realm? *What* is his realm? His realm is everywhere his authority extends and reaches. His realm is not limited to the church but extends beyond the church. Colossians 1:13 makes clear that Christ has a definite kingdom. When people are regenerated by the power of the Holy Spirit, they are most definitely brought into something that is real—"the kingdom of his beloved son." However, per Ephesians 1:22, all of creation is his realm. There is no place where Christ's authority does not extend. Nevertheless, his kingship appears to be mediatorial in that at

---

[24] Joel R. Beeke and Mark Jones, *A Puritan Theology: Doctrine for Life* (Grand Rapids, MI: Reformation Heritage Books, 2012), 356.

the last day, one of the final acts of Christ will be to turn everything over to his Father. Thus, while Christ is the king of the church, there is a time in which he hands everything, all authority and dominion, over to his heavenly Father. This is because all that the son does, he does for the glory of God the Father (John 17:4).

Approaching the King

While it is true that Christ calls his followers friends, brothers, and sisters, unfortunately these wonderful and comforting truths have been carried to their extremes. We are fond of remembering that Christ is our friend and brother, but forget that he is first our king, and that he continues to be king. Thankfully we are justified by faith alone in Christ alone and not by our right or wrong concept of his kingship, but the fact that our redemption and justification is based solely on the life, death, and resurrection of Christ should inspire us to greater reverence, not less. Sadly, the fact that Christ stepped out of the glories of heaven and took on human flesh and lived the perfect life of obedience to the Law of God on our behalf, so that those who place faith in Christ are imputed with his perfect righteousness by faith alone, and the fact that he died on the cross in our place to absorb the wrath of God on our behalf, has moved many Christians (particularly in the western world) to revere God less than the prophets and apostles did.

What we see in the New Testament is that those who became fully aware of the identity of Christ, or came to realize his kingship, approached him in commensurate manner. When the Magi came from the east in search of the newborn king, we are told "they saw the child with Mary his mother, and they fell down and worshiped him" (Matt. 2:11). They then presented him with gifts of gold, frankincense, and myrrh—gifts befitting a king.

When Jesus came across demon-possessed men and these demons suddenly realized they were standing in the presence of the king, they cried out in fear, 'What have you to do with us, Jesus, Son of the Most High God?!' (Matt. 8:29; Mark 1:24; 5:7). The demons understood that Jesus is king, that he has all authority in all of creation, and thus stood in his presence with fear and trembling. The demons demonstrated greater fear and reverence in Christ's presence than many Christians do today.

Throughout Jesus' life and ministry, the disciples often struggled to fully comprehend his nature and person. However, after his resurrection, when he met with the disciples, we read twice in Matthew 28 that they fell at his feet and worshiped him (vv.9, 17). On the one hand, they worshiped him because they came to understand his deity but, on the other hand, they paid tribute and honor to him as their king. We know that shortly after his resurrection, the disciples are still wondering if Jesus is now going to restore the kingdom to Israel (Acts 1:6). They recognized him as both God and King and, thus, entered his presence in appropriate manner.

When the apostle John is on the island of Patmos and hears a loud voice speaking behind him and turns to see from where the voice is coming and realizes he is standing in the presence of Christ, we read that he "fell at his feet as though dead" (Rev 1:17). And in chapter 5 we read that the four living creatures and the twenty-four elders fall down before the Lamb saying,

> "Worthy are you to take the scroll and to open its seals, for you were slain, and by your blood you ransomed people for God from every tribe and language and people and nation,

and you have made them a kingdom and priests to our God, and they shall reign on the earth." (Rev. 5:9-10)

It is worth noting that in all these circumstances whenever God's people found themselves in the presence of their king, they respond in a manner worthy of a king, and Christ does not say to them, 'Come on! Don't do that! We're just friends. It's really not that big of a deal.' Yet this is precisely the way many approach corporate worship on the Lord's Day. 'Come on! Jesus is my friend! It's really not that big of a deal!' To many, corporate worship is as important as watching a livestream of a royal wedding at Buckingham Palace. An extremely important moment to be sure, but *we are not actually there.* We are not *actually* in the king's presence and the king is not *actually* here, present with us. Many believe that in corporate worship Jesus is on his throne watching us from a distance, but he is not really here, present with us, and we are not really with him. *Nothing could be further from the truth.*

Chapter 6
Worshipping a Holy God

And whenever the living creatures give glory and honor and thanks to him who is seated on the throne, who lives forever and ever, the twenty-four elders fall down before him who is seated on the throne and worship him who lives forever and ever.
Revelation 4:9-10

The proper worship of God is inextricably linked to and derived from a proper understanding of God. Robert Dickie, in his wonderful little book *What the Bible Teaches About Worship*, points out that if we are ever going to worship God rightly, with reverence and awe, "we must make sure that our view of God is biblically accurate. To have defective views of who God is and what he has done will ensure that we will be wrong on how we worship and how we build the church."[25] Dickie is absolutely correct. Thus, it is imperative that we understand, first and foremost, that God is holy, holy, holy (Isa. 6:3; Rev. 4:8). He is a holy God who desires—*and commands*— that he be approached, treated, and worshiped in a holy, reverent, and sacred manner. Dickie goes on to make the following accurate assessment:

> Many people are worshipping a god that is a gross distortion of the God of the Bible. It is possible that many evangelicals may be guilty of a form of idolatry, worshipping a humanistic, man-made god. Some preachers and theologians are just as guilty as Aaron, who manufactured a golden calf for Israel to worship. When Aaron made the calf

---

[25] Robert L. Dickie, *What the Bible Teaches About Worship* (England: Evangelical Press, 2007), 100.

and brought it before the people, they said, 'This is your god, O Israel, that brought you out of the land of Egypt!' (Exodus 32:1-4 NKJV). Instead of worshipping the true and living God of Israel, Aaron encourages the people to worship a golden calf. This is idolatry! I believe that much of what passes for worship today is simply idolatry. We are not far removed from the error that Aaron made. We preach a strange and unbiblical god to our generation and then say, 'This is your God.'"[26]

Too many churches are concerned with '*what works.*' What will draw people into the church and what will keep them there? I do not wish to cast aspersions. Many of these churches are genuinely driven by the desire to reach the lost with the gospel and to see people come to Christ. However, in their zeal to see countless people come to worship God, they have inaccurately portrayed the God whom we worship. Who then is this God we worship and what is he like?

The Holiness of God

If one word were to be chosen which accurately describes the God of creation, that word would be *holy*. In Isaiah 6, when the prophet is given a glimpse into the very throne room of God as he gazes into the temple, God is so massive and so transcendent, we are told that Isaiah "saw the Lord sitting upon a throne, high and lifted up; and the train of his robe filled the temple." Isaiah was only able to see the "train of his robe." Picture the very end of God's robe folded over on itself, filling the temple. This would have reminded Isaiah of how small he

---

[26] Ibid., 100-101

is and just how massive and majestic God is. And as he is standing there like an ant staring up at a giant, he sees two seraphim (angels) high above and "one called to another and said: 'Holy, holy, holy is the LORD of hosts; the whole earth is full of his glory!'"[27] The angels in heaven throughout all eternity are constantly singing out one song to God-Almighty—"Holy, holy, holy, is the LORD of hosts."

We see a similar scene in the revelation God gave to John on the island of Patmos. In chapter four we read that John is allowed to see the very throne of God, and around the throne are four living creatures, "each of them with six wings, are full of eyes all around and within, and day and night they never cease to say, 'Holy, holy, holy, is the Lord God Almighty, who was and is and is to come!'" (v.8). Minimally, we learn three basic truths from Isaiah 6 and Revelation 4: (1) God is holy, holy, holy, (2) he loves to be worshiped and adored continuously, and (3) he never grows weary of hearing his holiness being exalted.[28] Regarding the three-fold refrain concerning God's holiness, however, R.C. Sproul in his classic book, *The Holiness of God*, rightly asserts, "Only once in sacred Scripture is an attribute of God elevated to the third degree. Only once is a characteristic of God mentioned three times in succession. The Bible says that God is holy, holy, holy. Not that He is merely holy, or even holy, holy. He is holy, holy, holy. The Bible never says that God is love, love, love, or mercy, mercy, mercy, or wrath, wrath,

---

[27] Since Isaiah could only see the train of God's robe, then clearly the seraphim were not hovering above the head of God but were hovering high above the train of his robe. A more accurate translation from the Hebrew might be: "Above it [the train of his robe] stood seraphim" (see YLT, KJV).
[28] If there was ever an argument to be made from scripture for the use of repetitive choruses being sung in corporate worship, this might be it.

wrath, or justice, justice, justice. It does say he is holy, holy, holy, the whole earth is full of His glory" [*sic*].[29]

Hence, if there is one word that can be chosen from scripture to describe God in his totality, that word is *holy*. Ironically, I believe if a survey were taken, and most Christians were asked to offer one word to describe God, most would say *love*. Of course, their answer is not unfounded. Twice in the epistle of 1 John, the apostle makes the statement that "God is love" (4:8, 16). Yet, as Sproul pointed out, the Bible never says God is love, love, love, or even that he is love, love. But twice we are told that God is *holy, holy, holy*. Then why do so many Christians overlook the holiness of God and focus on the love of God? It may be that God's love is easier to take in, easier to embrace. The holiness of God is not. When people hear that God is love, that God loves you, it gives them warm fuzzies. What they hear is that God makes no demands on their lives. As the old hymn goes, "Just as I am, without one plea..." But when people hear talk about the holiness of God, they react much the same way Isaiah did, "Woe is me! For I am lost; for I am a man of unclean lips, and I dwell in the midst of a people of unclean lips." Or, they respond the way Peter did when he suddenly realized he was standing in the presence of holiness. "Depart from me, for I am a sinful man, O Lord" (Lk. 5:8). In other words, the perception of many evangelicals (wrongly so) is that the holiness of God makes demands on our lives; God's love does not. Both the holiness of God and the love of God make demands. They both demand a particular response from the creature—*humble and reverent worship*.

---

[29] R.C. Sproul, *The Holiness of God* (Wheaton, IL: Tyndale House Publishers, 1985), 39.

But what does it mean that God is *holy*, that he is *holy, holy, holy*? In answering this question, Gentry makes the following statement: "Unfortunately, the church of Jesus Christ, at least in the western world, has not understood very well the meaning of the word holy, nor what it means to worship a holy God."[30] He goes on to say that one can "see from careful exegesis of scripture, neither 'moral purity' nor 'transcendence' are fundamental to the meaning of holy either in Greek or in Hebrew. The best approach to semantic analysis is an exhaustive study of all available usage, not only for the literature in question, but also for the contemporary documents in the cultures surrounding the original texts of the Bible."[31]

Accordingly, what it means for someone or something to be holy is for that someone or something to be dedicated or devoted for some higher purpose and meaning. This is seen in the Exodus account of Moses meeting with God at the burning bush. As Moses becomes curious about the bush that is on fire but not being consumed and begins to move toward it, God speaks to him and says, "Do not come near; take your sandals off your feet, for the place on which you are standing is holy ground." What does it mean for the ground to be holy? If we understand holy in the traditional sense of *moral purity* or *uprightness*, then we must ask in what way is the ground Moses is standing on morally pure or upright? Dirt is morally neutral, neither good nor evil. If we understand holy to mean *separateness*, we are still left with unanswered questions. How is the ground Moses is standing separate from the surrounding ground that is still connected to it? Where does the separateness begin and end? And why is Moses not called holy, but only the ground upon

---

[30] Gentry, "No One *Holy* Like the Lord," 17.
[31] Ibid., 20.

which he is standing is considered holy? "We can recognize then, in Exodus 3, a meaning of a derivative of the root *qdš* [holy] current in the 14th century before Jesus Christ, where the *qdš* ground is not the place of distance or radical separation, but of meeting and of presence, the meeting of God and man."[32] What makes the ground holy where Moses is standing is that it is the dedicated meeting place between God and Moses. It is a parcel of ground that is devoted to God for his purpose, use, and glory. We see then that when the Bible speaks of God being holy, holy, holy, it means that God is wholly and completely devoted to himself, to his name, to his own glory, honor, and worship. Everything God does is ultimately and always for his own glory. God is holy, holy, holy.

The Holiness of God's Possessions

Throughout the Old Testament, things, places, people, and groups of people chosen by God and devoted to him and for his glory are considered holy to God. Jerusalem was considered a holy city as it was thought to be the city of God (Neh. 11:1; Ps. 46:4). This is not to say that God did not exist anywhere else or that he could not be prayed to and worshiped outside of Jerusalem. But Jerusalem was the one city that was to be specifically devoted to Yahweh and to his worship and glory. It was the place where the house of the LORD was to be established; the designated meeting place between God and his people (2 Chron. 36:14). Thus, we see that the temple and all its furnishings were thought to be holy to the LORD. Holy, not in the sense of having *moral purity* or *uprightness*, nor in the sense

---

[32] Ibid., 22.

of simply being set apart for God, but rather the temple and its furnishings were devoted *to God* and *for God*.

We see the concept of holiness also being applied to the people of Israel. As they come out of Egyptian bondage and are making their way across the wilderness to the promised land, God says to them, "For you are a people holy to the LORD your God. The LORD your God has chosen you to be a people for his treasured possession, out of all the peoples who are on the face of the earth" (Deut. 7:6). Israel was a people who were to be completely devoted to the worship and glory of Yahweh, which is evident from the first two commandments of the decalogue. "You shall have no other gods before me;" and "you shall not make for yourself any graven image and bow down to them." The people of Israel were to be completely devoted to the God who delivered them from slavery. God had redeemed them for that very purpose, that they might be utterly devoted to God and to his glory just as much as God was wholly devoted to himself and to his own glory.

Within the nation of Israel there was one tribe that was to be even more devoted to God than all the others—the Levites. They were to be so devoted to God and to rightly worshipping him that they were not to possess their own land for God was their possession and treasure (Num. 18:20). The Levites, at least those who served as priests, were to devote the whole of their lives to serving God and to ministering within his temple (Lev. 21:6). In this sense, they were holy, devoted to God. To be sure, not every Levite served as a priest, but every priest was to be a Levite. Hence, in some sense the Levitical priests were to be different from the rest of the nation. Although they were Jewish, they were to live differently and were to worship differently than everyone else (Lev. 21:1-22:16).

Like the Levites, in the New Testament we see that believers have been chosen out of the world. During Jesus' high priestly prayer, he says to the Father, "I have given them your word, and the world has hated them because they are not of the world, just as I am not of the world. I do not ask that you take them out of the world, but that you keep them from the evil one. They are not of the world, just as I am not of the world...I do not ask for these only, but also for those who will believe in me through their word," (John 17:14-16, 20). Believers are holy to God. This is reinforced by the fact that throughout the epistles, God's people are regularly referred to as '*the holy ones*.' In most of the epistles found in the New Testament we see the address being made "to the saints" (*hagios* = holy). Followers of Christ are also said to be a "royal priesthood, a holy nation, a people for his own possession" (1 Pet. 2:9). This is language that is steeped in the Old Testament Levitical priesthood. God's people, Old and New Testament, are to live lives which are wholly and completely devoted to God, to his worship, and to his glory.

In clarifying the distinction between 'holy' as *separateness* and 'holy' as *devotedness*, Case is most helpful when he writes,

Although our devotion to God will involve separating ourselves from certain things and striving to be blameless, they are not equal concepts, just as loving one's wife is not the same as avoiding pornography (even though it should include that). The one is positive and the other negative. What we want to communicate is the positive and fundamental aspect of holiness, wherein God pours himself out for the good of his people, and people offer their hands and hearts to God and his glory.[33]

God's people are called to be holy and to pursue holiness in that they are called to live wholly devoted to God and to his glory.

Chosen to Worship a Holy God

We could learn a lot from the heavenly hosts with regards to the proper manner with which the creature should worship the Creator. In Isaiah 6, when the prophet sees the seraphim flying and worshipping God, he says "with two he covered his face, and with two he covered his feet, and with two he flew." Like Moses, whom God did not allow to see his face (Ex. 33:20), the angels covered their faces so as not to gaze upon the face and glory of God, though they are not sinful creatures. In many eastern cultures it is considered disrespectful and defiant for children to look into the face of their parents or for adults to look into the face of their superiors. Hence, the bowing of heads and looking down when being addressed by someone in greater authority. Hence, the angels covered their faces as an outward sign of reverence and submission.

They also covered their feet as an outward sign of reverence and submission to their Creator. Feet—the removing of sandals from one's feet (Ex. 3), the washing of one's feet (John 13), the kissing of one's feet (Lk. 7), the hiding of one's feet (Isa. 6)—are a symbol of humility and creatureliness. The covering of their feet demonstrates their awareness of "the depth at which

---

[33] Andrew Case, "Towards a Better Understanding of God's Holiness: Challenging the Status Quo," *The Bible Translator*, 2017; 68(3):269-283. doi:10.1177/2051677017728565, pg. 282.

the creature stands below the Holiest of all,..."[34] Thus, the angels in heaven cover their faces and cover their feet in the presence of God, and as they worship Him.

In Revelation 4, we are told that whenever the angels sing "holy, holy, holy, is the Lord God Almighty," the twenty-four elders in heaven "fall down before him who is seated on the throne and worship him" (v.10). The identity of the twenty-four elders is not significant for my point. The point is that like the host of heaven, God's people have been chosen, called, and redeemed to worship a holy God. The hosts of heaven do not merely worship the King with reverence and awe in their minds and hearts. They externally display reverence and awe as they engage in the worship of God Almighty. They know in whose presence they stand and worship, and they respond accordingly. This should not be overlooked.

Of course, the worship of God is not something that only happens on Sunday morning. Scripture says, "I appeal to you therefore, brothers, by the mercies of God, to present your bodies as a living sacrifice, holy and acceptable to God, which is your spiritual worship" (Rom. 12:1). Thus, the way in which we offer spiritual worship to God is by presenting our "bodies as a living sacrifice, holy and acceptable to God." God created his people, called and redeemed them, for his glory (Isa. 43:6-7). As we seek to live for the glory of God, as we strive to pursue holiness (Heb. 12:14) and to honor our Creator in all that we do, we are living lives of worship. In one sense, worship is to be lived out in all of life, in everything we do, say, and think.

However, in another sense, heavenly worship before the throne of God takes place when the saints gather for corporate

---

[34] C.F. Keil and F. Delitzsch, Commentary on the Old Testament (Peabody, MA: Hendrickson Publishers, 1866-91; reprint, 2006), 7:124.

worship. In Ephesians 2, Paul tells his Gentile readers that they are "fellow citizens with the saints and members of the household of God" and as fellow citizens and members of the household of God, they are being joined together into a "holy temple in the Lord" (vv.19-21). Peter tells us that each believer is a "living stone", which when brought together comprise a "spiritual house" for God (1 Pet. 2:4-5). "Public worship is the entrance of believers into the special presence of the Triune God, on terms which He has stipulated, for the purpose of covenant renewal, by means of the Spirit's power to effect the believer's participation in the Son's communion with the Father."[35] The gathering of the saints on the Lord's Day for corporate worship is the most important event any person can participate in, anywhere, anytime, in anyplace. The significance of corporate worship far exceeds any wedding in the grandest cathedral, any audience with the most powerful monarch, or any invitation to dine at the White House. "Christians actually [and] spiritually ascend to heaven through the ordained means of corporate worship—God's Word and the Sacraments. Public worship, and particularly the Lord's Supper, is likened to a ladder which raises the elect up to the presence of Christ in heaven."[36]

That God is holy, his people are holy, and the place of corporate worship is holy, means that he is to be worshiped in a way that is different from the world, a way that is completely devoted (*holy*) to him, not common or ordinary. Everything about the worship service should look and feel different from the world. And it will, if corporate worship is done in accordance with scripture. In Deuteronomy 12:29-32, just as Israel is

---

[35] Kelley, "Seated in the Heavenlies," 16-17.
[36] Ibid., 97.

preparing to enter the promised land, Moses gives them the following instructions:

> When the LORD your God cuts off before you the nations whom you go in to dispossess, and you dispossess them and dwell in their land, take care that you be not ensnared to follow them, after they have been destroyed before you, and that you do not inquire about their gods, saying, 'How did these nations serve their gods?—that I also may do the same.' You shall not worship the LORD your God in that way, …Everything that I command you, you shall be careful to do. You shall not add to it or take from it.

The people of Israel were not to look to the inhabitants of the land of Canaan and borrow from them with regards to the worship of God. They were to worship God in exactly the way he had commanded them. They were not to add anything to what God had commanded regarding his worship, nor were they to subtract anything from it. This desire of God still holds firm today, as we will see more clearly in the next chapter. But corporate worship should not look like a rock concert, a drama theater, a town hall meeting, or a conference lecture. Rather, what is done in corporate worship, and the way we enter corporate worship, should reflect the holiness of the One we worship, the One who has called us to be holy, just as he is holy. To have a wrong view of the God we worship will inevitably lead to wrong worship. God is our friend, and he is our heavenly Father, but above all—*He is our God and King.*

To treat God in a manner less than holy can have dire consequences. When the people grumbled against Moses and Aaron because there was no water to drink, they went before the Lord and asked what to do. God clearly and specifically commands Moses to "Take the staff, and assemble the

112

congregation, you and Aaron your brother, and tell the rock before their eyes to yield its water. So you shall bring water out of the rock for them and give drink to the congregation and their cattle" (Num. 20:8). But instead, Moses says to the people, "'Hear now, you rebels: shall we bring water for you out of this rock?' And Moses lifted up his hand and struck the rock with his staff twice, and water came out abundantly, and the congregation drank, and their livestock." There are two tragic mistakes Moses committed. First, he robbed God of his due glory when he said, "Shall we bring water for you out of this rock?" *Shall we?* What is this '*we*' business? Moses claims partial credit for bringing forth water from the rock. Second, in his frustration he strikes the rock twice with his staff. God did not command Moses to strike the rock. He merely told him to speak to it. For these reasons God says to Moses and Aaron, "Because you did not believe in me, *to uphold me as holy* in the eyes of the people of Israel, therefore you shall not bring this assembly into the land that I have given them" [emphasis added]. In their disobedience and lack of faith, in their not following through with what God had specifically commanded, they did not treat God as holy.

We witness a similar event with Aaron's two sons, Nadab and Abihu (Lev. 10). They take it upon themselves to offer "unauthorized fire before the LORD, which he had not commanded them" to do and God consumes them in fire. This may seem harsh, but Moses says to Aaron, "It is what the LORD spoke, saying, 'By those who come near Me *I will be treated as holy*, and before all the people I will be honored'" (NASB, emphasis added). God demands—even today—that he be treated and worshiped as holy by those who come near him.

Five-hundred years later, Uzzah would make a similar and fatal mistake (2 Sam. 6). As King David was moving the Ark of the Covenant up Mt. Zion to Jerusalem, he had it placed on an ox cart. This was the first mistake. God had commanded that the Ark be carried on the shoulders of the Levites via two poles, for no human was ever allowed to touch the Ark of God—the throne of God (Ex. 37:4). Yet as the ox cart is moving up the hill, the oxen stumble and Uzzah reaches out his hand to stabilize the Ark to prevent it from sliding off the cart and crashing to the ground, and God strikes him dead. There is a clear message being communicated from this event. Voddie Baucham rightly states: "God essentially says to us through killing Uzzah, 'This is not about what you want or what you feel. This is about what I say.'"[37] It did not matter that Uzzah had the best intentions. God desires to be treated as holy, demonstrated through obedience and reverence. Far too often we think of God as *abba* (daddy), our friend, our pal, our amigo, and we forget who he truly is. He is *El-Shaddai* (God-Almighty), *El-elyon* (God Most High), the one who spoke the universe into existence by the power of his word. He is the self-existent one, a consuming fire, the great I Am. He is the King above all kings and the Lord above all lords. He is holy, holy, holy!

This in mind, God's place of worship—the corporate gathering of the saints—ought to be treated as holy, reverent, sacred, and special. There is no event on earth, no place on the face of the planet, that is more important, that carries more gravitas, than the gathering of God's people for corporate worship. When God's people gather for *church*, and all the biblical and necessary elements are present for there to be a true

---

[37] Voddie Baucham, cited in *The Church Bible Study Set*, disc 1, timestamp 1:21:05.

church, God's presence is there in their midst in a more significant way than he is anywhere else. God is just as present amid our corporate worship as he was to Moses in the burning bush, to the Israelites at Mt. Sinai, or to Isaiah within the temple. Just as when Moses stood in the presence of God before the burning bush, God was still present *everywhere else*, but his presence where Moses was standing was more significant than *anywhere else*—and Moses recognized it. We should too.

Chapter 7
Throne Room Decorum

> *I have applied all these things to myself and Apollos for your benefit, brothers, that you may learn by us not to go beyond what is written, that none of you may be puffed up in favor of one against another.*
> 1 Corinthians 4:6

One thing my wife and I have always made a point of doing, throughout our marriage, is to attend church whenever we are traveling. As young believers, we were discipled regarding the importance of church attendance (Heb. 10:24-25). God instituted the visible church, the place of corporate worship, the designated meeting place between God and his people, as a means of grace, a place for our souls to be nourished and fed, a place where the saints might encourage and admonish one another, a place where we might hear from God.

However, we also just thoroughly enjoy attending church and worshipping with the saints and hearing God's word proclaimed. We have always struggled to understand how Christians can sleep in on Sunday morning. Even when we have gotten to bed very late for various reasons, we always made it a point to be there on Sunday. I am not boasting. I am not sharing this information as a way of displaying my personal holiness. Rather, like the avid fisherman who is willing to sacrifice sleep and wake up at some ungodly hour in order to get the best spot on the lake *simply because he loves fishing*, occasionally having to sacrifice sleep in order to do what we love most has always been a small price to pay.

But since my seminary days, we have also enjoyed visiting different kinds of churches, fellowships from different denominations. This started when I was taking a seminary class on church worship. As part of the course requirements, during the semester the students were expected to attend three different types of worship services from what they were accustomed to, and then write a reflection paper describing the church worship service. At the time, I was attending a Baptist seminary. I cannot remember the third church, as that was many years ago, but I do remember visiting a predominantly African American Pentecostal church and a high-liturgical Lutheran church. Having been raised Roman Catholic, the Lutheran church made me feel as though I had been transported back to my childhood. Nevertheless, I found both the Pentecostal church and the Lutheran church to be a great blessing to me and a very enjoyable time of worship. Since then, my wife and I have often tried to find different kinds of evangelical churches to attend when traveling.

What we have found interesting, however, and probably not news to most Christians, is all the various ways in which church worship services are conducted. It can lead one to think that the Bible must have nothing to say about corporate worship. The various worship styles seem to, as Horton notes, "substantiate the prevailing assumption that how we worship is simply a matter of style, not substance—never mind the second commandment, which prescribes not only whom we worship but how he wants to be worshiped."[38] The myriad of ways churches worship can lead some to think that God has left it up to our devices, preferences, imagination, and cultural norms to determine what we should or should not do in corporate worship.

---

[38] Michael Horton, *A Better Way: Rediscovering the Drama of Christ-Centered Worship* (Grand Rapids, MI: Baker Books, 2002) 11.

The Sufficiency of God's Word

In his classic work, *He Is There and He Is Not Silent*, Francis Schaeffer asks the question:

> In the Christian structure, would it be unlikely that this personal God who is there and made man in His own image as a verbalizer, in such a way that he can communicate horizontally to other men on the basis of propositions and languages—is it unthinkable or even surprising that this personal God could or would communicate to man on the basis of propositions? The answer is, no. I have never met an atheist who thought that this would be regarded as surprising within the Christian structure. Indeed, it is what one would expect.[39]

Not only is this what one would expect, but this is precisely what has happened. The God of creation is a speaking God. He is a God who communicates, not just with his creation, but among and within the Godhead. The Father, Son, and Holy Spirit have always communicated with each other throughout eternity (John 6:38-39; 17:4). God has also communicated with his creation. Beginning in the garden of Eden and throughout redemptive history, God speaks and reveals himself, reveals his desires, and his demands. "Long ago, at many times and in many ways, God spoke to our fathers by the prophets, but in these last days he has spoken to us by his Son, whom he appointed the heir of all things, through whom also he created the world" (Heb. 1:1-2).

God continues to speak to us today, authoritatively and infallibly, through his word. "All Scripture is breathed out by God and profitable for teaching, for reproof, for correction, and

---

[39] Ibid., 325.

for training in righteousness, that the man of God may be complete, equipped for every good work" (2 Tim. 3:16-17). The words "breathed out by God" in the underlying Greek is one word—*theopneustos*—and this is the only occurrence in the entire Bible. It is a compound word comprised of the words for God, *theos*, and the verb "to breathe," *ekpneō*. Thus, all scripture is the very breath of God. Just as when a person is speaking closely to us, there is breath coming forth from his or her mouth. Scripture is not merely a record of what God has spoken—*scripture is God speaking*. Scripture is the breath of God. Through the power of the Holy Spirit, when God's people read his word, God is speaking to us in the here and now. Through scripture, in a very real sense, we hear what the prophets in the Old Testament heard—*the voice of God*.

For this reason, Peter tells us in 2 Peter 1:3 that God's "divine power has granted to us all things that pertain to life and godliness, through the knowledge of him who called us..." In other words, everything we need to know which "pertain to life" (i.e., living in this world) and "godliness" (i.e., growing in sanctification and worshipping God rightly) has been given to us "through the knowledge of [God] who called us". The more we study God, the more we study the things of God, the more we learn about God, the more time we spend in His word, the more we will know what God requires of us and how he desires to be worshiped.

To ensure his point is not missed or minimized, Peter goes on to explain (vv.16-21) that he and the other apostles did not make this stuff up but that they were with Jesus "on the holy mountain" (Matt. 17:1-8) when they heard the voice "borne to him by the Majestic Glory, 'This is my beloved Son, with whom I am well pleased'". In terms of evidence and assurance of who

Jesus is, what could be more reassuring than being on the mountain with Jesus and hearing the voice of God speak from the cloud? Yet, Peter says that we who are alive today, post-ascension, "have something more sure" (v.19), something more certain, reliable, and trustworthy. We have "the prophetic word", Holy Scripture, "to which you will do well to pay attention as to a lamp shining in a dark place,..." How is it that Peter is able to say that scripture is "more sure," more certain, than being on the holy mountain with Jesus and hearing the voice of God? He believes this because "no prophecy of Scripture comes from someone's own interpretation. For no prophecy was ever produced by the will of man, *but men spoke from God as they were carried along by the Holy Spirit.*" Because scripture is the product of men speaking from God as they were carried along by the Holy Spirit and because all scripture is God-breathed (*theopneustos*), then all scripture is the very word of God, the very instruction of God. The scriptures are sufficient to communicate to us everything we need to know regarding God and how he desires to be worshiped.

Part of what has led to this casual, *anything-goes*, form of worship we see in many churches today is a low view of scripture. Many view scripture not as God speaking directly to us in the here and now, but rather as a rough guide that we need not slavishly follow. Yes, the Bible was given by divine inspiration but for many, "divine inspiration" means that the writers were emotionally moved by the Holy Spirit to write a religious book, much the way Leonardo da Vinci was inspired to paint the *Mona Lisa*. Yet, Paul writes to Timothy, whom he has left in Ephesus to shepherd the church there, "I write so that you may know how one ought to conduct himself in the household of God, which is the church of the living God, the pillar and support of the truth" (1 Tim. 3:15 NASB). Paul wrote to Timothy so that the church might know "how one ought to conduct himself in the household of God". If more Christians understood that the things which Paul wrote "are a command of the Lord" (1 Cor. 14:37), that all scripture is "God-breathed," they would pay closer attention to what scripture has to say about corporate worship—about how one ought to conduct himself in the household of God. The church is the household of God. It is God's house. When we enter God's house, we ought to conduct ourselves and conduct our worship in a way which he desires, in a way he has prescribed.

What Scripture Commands Regarding Worship

Once again, allow me to remind the reader that as the Israelites were moving across the wilderness, and as they were preparing to enter the land of Canaan, Moses, under the divine inspiration of the Holy Spirit, gave them these words:

> When the LORD your God cuts off before you the nations whom you go in to dispossess, and you dispossess them and dwell in their land, take care that you be not ensnared to follow them, after they have been destroyed before you, and that you do not inquire about their gods, saying, 'How did these nations serve their gods?—that I also may do the same.' You shall not worship the LORD your God in that way, for every abominable thing that the LORD hates they have done for their gods, for they even burn their sons and their daughters in the fire to their gods. Everything that I command you, you shall be careful to do. You shall not add to it or take from it. (Deut. 12:29-32)

There are two important points worth noting from this passage. First, the Israelites were not to borrow from the people of the land regarding the worship of God. They were not to try and incorporate the practices of the pagan world into the worship of Yahweh, no matter how unique, interesting or different it may be. Yet this is precisely what many evangelical churches are and have been doing for many decades. In their effort to offer a *unique worship experience* and to make Christianity attractive to the unbelieving world, they look out at the world to see what they can borrow from the corporate world and from the fast-growing megachurches. Before the first coming of Christ, God expressly forbade his people from borrowing from the world. Why should we think things would be any different for his people before his second coming?

A second important point worth noting is that God explicitly states, "Everything that I command you, you shall be careful to do. You shall not add to it or take from it." In its context, God is clearly speaking about worship. God is to be worshiped in the way he has commanded. God's people were not to add anything to it nor were they to subtract anything from it. To be sure, we are talking about the Old Testament era, and we know that much of the way they worshiped in the Old Testament era does not carry over into the New Testament era due to the coming of Christ and his fulfillment of the Law (Matt. 5:17; Gal. 3:19-26). Nevertheless, Sproul rightly notes that we "behave as if nothing God said on the subject of worship in the Old Testament applies today. If we are to come back to the foundation, if we are to please God in our worship, does it not make sense to ask whether there has ever been a time when the unchanging God Himself revealed the kind of worship that was pleasing to Him?"[40] The answer is unequivocally yes! If God demands his people only

---

[40] Sproul, *How Then Shall We Worship?*, 18.

worship him in the manner which he prescribes, and God is "the same yesterday and today and forever" (Heb. 13:8), then it stands to reason that he demands, even today, that his people worship him in the manner which he himself has prescribed.

In fact, Paul begins his letter to the church in Corinth by reminding them of this important biblical truth. Yes, the church in Corinth was a mess and they were dealing with all sorts of theological and interpersonal problems and, yes, Paul wrote the letter to help them sort through these problems and get them on the right track, but rather than view the first epistle to the church in Corinth as a letter about Paul helping the church straighten out their mess, the letter can more rightly be viewed as being about what a biblical church looks like, functions like, and worships like. Thus, near the beginning of 1 Corinthians, Paul offers himself and Apollos as examples to the church "that you may learn by us not to go beyond what is written" (4:6). Of course, what Paul means by "what is written" is a point of debate. He either means (1) what he has written thus far in 1 Cor. 1:1-4:5, (2) the entire letter of 1 Corinthians, (3) the letter he previously wrote to the Corinthians [see 1 Cor 5:9], or (4) what is written in the Old Testament, the only Bible they had at the time. However, regardless of what Paul meant by "what is written", here is what is clear—they were *not to go beyond what is written.*" Whether Paul is speaking about his own writings or the writings of the Old Testament, when it comes to how a biblical church is to function and worship, how Christians are to behave and live their lives, we must not go beyond what is written. We must not go beyond Holy Scripture. We must not use our creativity or imagination or borrow from the world or from the megachurches or do '*what works*' to determine how to worship God, how to engage in corporate worship.

In scripture, our King has made clear how he is to be worshiped, what is proper and acceptable decorum when entering his throne room. Every king in every nation throughout the history of the world has a set of do's and don'ts when entering into his presence, when entering into his throne room. And not just kings, we all have certain expectations of people who come into our home and, regardless of who they are (friend or family), we would be offended if they refused to abide by our expectations. Not long ago I went to visit with a family in our church who recently moved to the United States from South Korea. When I entered their living room, I chatted with them for a few moments and then the wife looked down at my feet and kindly asked if I would remove my shoes. Of course, I immediately complied. I would not want to be disrespectful to my hosts in their own home. The visible church is God's house. She is God's church—not our church, not the pastor's church—God's church.

How Scripture Guides Us Regarding Worship
Looking out at the landscape of corporate worship, Horton rightly observes:
The assumption these days often seems to be that God has not said anything about how we should worship him. For instance, some have argued that a weekly service need not include the preaching of the Word, as God can speak his Word through a variety of other instruments: drama, liturgical dance, poetry, and so on. Repeatedly, worship is reduced to a matter of consumer tastes. One person prefers

guitars, another prefers organs: Isn't that all this debate is about?[41]

Is that all this debate is about—*preferences*? Is that all we are really talking about? Most Christians, if not all, would agree that the Bible ought to provide some guide which governs our worship. The question becomes: How and to what extent? How does the Bible provide us guidance to worship? That is, how limiting is the Bible when it comes to corporate worship?

There are essentially two schools of thought when it comes to the question of how the Bible regulates corporate worship. The normative principle of worship and the regulative principle of worship. Whether or not Christians or churches have heard of these terms or are familiar with them, all Christians, all evangelical churches, fall into one of these two camps when it comes to determining how the Bible governs how we should engage in the corporate worship of God.

The normative principle of worship teaches that Christians must minimally do that which scripture explicitly commands to be done in worship (pray, preach, sing, etc.), but are also free to do that which scripture does not expressly forbid and does not violate the clear teachings of scripture. This view of corporate worship is practiced by such organizations as Lutherans, Anglicans, Methodists, Episcopalians, and most charismatic, independent Baptists, and Bible churches. It's the idea that so long as our heart is in the right place, so long as our motives are pure, so long as our desire is to honor God, minister to the saints, and reach the lost with the gospel, it does not really matter how we worship God so long as we are not violating the clear

---

[41] Horton, *A Better Way*, 29.

teachings of scripture and so long as we are doing the bare essentials of what scripture commands.

For this reason, in high liturgical churches, you may see the minister dressed like the Pope and swinging incense. In low liturgical churches, you may see fog machines during the worship singing and confetti being blown through the air vents.[42] In both instances one might ask, 'Where are they getting that from?' I don't see the New Testament church swinging incense or turning the lights down low and using fog machines during worship. Those who ascribe to the normative principle of worship would say that neither does the Bible expressly forbid the use of these things. Thus, these are left to the preferences of individuals and of individual churches and denominations. However, though the Bible does not expressly forbid the use of these and other inventions, in Deuteronomy 12:32 and 1 Corinthians 4:6 God is quite clear. "Everything that I command you, you shall be careful to do. You shall not add to it or take from it" and churches are "not to go beyond what is written…" When it comes to the worship of God, we dare not add to or subtract from that which God has commanded in his word.

The other camp that churches fall into is what is known as the regulative principle of worship. This view is succinctly explained quite well in the Westminster Confession of Faith which states: "The acceptable way of worshipping the true God

---

[42] The word *liturgy* simply means 'order of worship.' Every church has a liturgy, a way of conducting worship. Churches with '*high liturgical worship*' are churches which might be described as having very formal and traditional worship, for example Anglicans and Lutherans. Churches with '*low liturgical worship*' are churches which might be described as having very informal or casual worship. Thus, 'low liturgical worship' is not derogatory, but is simply a term for describing a church's style and theological view of worship.

is instituted by Himself, and so limited by His own revealed will, that He may not be worshiped according to the imaginations and devices of men, or the suggestions of Satan, under any visible representation, or any other way not prescribed in the Holy Scripture."[43] That last clause alone nicely sums up the point—"*any other way not prescribed in the Holy Scripture.*" In other words, as the name implies, the regulative principle of worship argues that scripture alone should *regulate* what is and is not done in corporate worship. God, our great King, has expressly and explicitly given commands as to how he is to be worshiped and approached, "all of which are either expressly set down in Scripture, or by good and necessary inference may be deduced therefrom; and to which things He commands that nothing be added, and that from them naught be taken away."[44] What we do in corporate worship, how we do corporate worship, the order in which we conduct corporate worship, the manner in which we enter into corporate worship, ought to be either expressly prescribed by scripture or be clearly deduced from it.

It's no coincidence that at the end of the cannon, John pens these words: "I warn everyone who hears the words of the prophecy of this book: if anyone adds to them, God will add to him the plagues described in this book, and if anyone takes away from the words of the book of this prophecy, God will take away his share in the tree of life and in the holy city, which are described in this book" (Rev. 22:18-19). To be sure, when John wrote those words, he was referring to the letter which he had just written to the seven churches in Asia. But surely John's warning can be applied to all Holy Scripture. We must not think

---

[43] *The Westminster Confession of Faith* (1646), 21:1.
[44] *The Book of Church Order of the Presbyterian Church in America* (2007), Preface, Section I, para. 4.

it is only the book of Revelation we are not to add or subtract anything from. When it comes to corporate worship, churches would be wise to take the apostle John's warning to heart.

Chapter 8
Inside the Throne Room

I am writing these things to you so that, if I delay, you may know how one ought to behave in the household of God, which is the church of the living God, a pillar and buttress of the truth.
1 Timothy 3:14-15

When we argue for the regulative principle of worship and say that what we do in corporate worship must be clearly derived from scripture, inevitably the debate turns to what *exactly* must be derived from scripture? For example, the Bible says nothing about the use of pulpits or chairs or overhead projectors or sound equipment. We also know that the New Testament church met in homes throughout the city, not in a centralized church building. Thus, how far do we carry the regulative principle?

Even among those who ascribe to the regulative principle, there is debate as to what constitutes a biblical and necessary element of worship and what does not. Does the regulative principle necessitate strict psalmody? May instruments be used in worship? If so, what kinds of instruments? May we only use pipe organ or only piano? Must we only sing hymns, or may contemporary music be used? Must the Lord's Supper be taken every week, once a month, once a quarter? And should it be taken during the morning service or evening service?

Here Doug Wilson is quite right when he states that the "question of consistency has to be addressed here because strict regulativists are quite arbitrary in their pronouncement on what stays and what goes. Examined closely, it is not the regulative *principle* which is winnowing the wheat and chaff, but rather the personality types of the regulativists themselves."[45] To be fair, if one were to move from one regulative church to another, the churches would not be identical in worship styles. One would notice some differences, but the differences would be subtle. A noticeable continuity would and does exist among regulative churches. Thus, for the purpose and scope of this book, I will leave many stones unturned. Strictly speaking, this is not a book on *the regulative principle*. Rather, this is a book about the meaning and spiritual reality of corporate worship, and how churches and individuals should approach corporate worship. Scripture alone should determine how one approaches and engages in corporate worship, over and against those who argue that scripture *plus cultural norms* should determine what we do in corporate worship.

On this point Horton is most helpful when he writes that "while God has commanded us to gather together on the Lord's Day, he has not commanded us to meet at 10:00. Church services will vary in entirely appropriate ways; some things are necessary while other things depend on circumstances of time and place. The former we ordinarily call an *element* (i.e., it is necessary), while the latter is a *circumstance* (i.e., it is up to the church's discretion). Taking an offering is an element, while how it is taken is a circumstance."[46] Gathering for church is an *element*. Where we gather for church (a home, a gym, a church building) is a *circumstance*. Reading God's word is an *element*. What we read God's word from (an overhead screen or the bulletin) is a *circumstance*.

---

[45] Douglas Wilson, *Mother Kirk: Essays and Forays in Practical Ecclesiology* (Moscow, ID: Canon Press, 2001), 122.
[46] Horton, *A Better Way*, 148.

The Elements of Corporate Worship

When we talk about the elements of corporate worship, we are discussing what must be done in corporate worship, what God prescribes and what can be logically deduced from scripture.

Prayer. In 1 Timothy 2:1-2, Paul issues the following command to Timothy:

> First of all, then, I urge that supplications, prayers, intercessions, and thanksgivings be made for all people, for kings and all who are in high positions, that we may lead a peaceful and quiet life, godly and dignified in every way.

Keep in mind that Timothy had been left in Ephesus to shepherd the church which Paul had planted. Thus, Paul had written this letter to instruct Timothy on how to conduct church, how the church is to function and behave in corporate worship, and he commands him to pray and intercede and give thanks for "all people, for kings and all who are in high positions." Thus, we are not simply to pray for our political leaders, but we are to pray for "all people."

Prayer in church, however, just makes sense. Prayer is the creature's way of humbly acknowledging our dependence on the Creator and our need for his help, strength, and guidance. To not saturate the worship service with prayer is to imply our independence from God and that God is most concerned with external rituals, not internal affections and heartfelt dependance on him.

Praying in church is also a way of teaching our members how to pray. Quite often one of the most difficult things for new believers to engage in is prayer. They struggle to know how to pray or what to pray for. For these reasons, it is beneficial to the members that the church engages in much prayer during corporate worship and pray for a variety of different things and people. The service should begin with a *Prayer of Invocation*. As the title suggests, the prayer of invocation is a time of invoking God's blessing upon the service. At a point in the liturgy, usually after the Reading of the Law, I lead our church through a *Prayer of Confession*. This is a time of prayer in our church worship service when we reflect upon the scripture reading we have just heard, and we reflect upon all that our God and king requires of us. At some point during the prayer, I will usually pause for about 30 seconds to allow our church members to confess their transgressions privately to God in their minds. This is an opportunity to confess to God that we have sinned throughout the week and to acknowledge and confess those specific sins so that we might worship God and partake of the Lord's Supper in a worthy manner (1 Cor. 11:27).

This is followed by the *Assurance of Pardon* scripture reading, which is then followed by our *Prayer of Intercession*. By "intercession" I mean that the church collectively is praying together for various items of the church and world, *interceding* on their behalf, with one person leading the prayer. The prayer of intercession might include a time where the church praises and thanks God for his many blessings, confesses their sins to God and asks his forgiveness, and prays for the spiritual health of the church, a specific ministry within the church, several families within the church, a missionary family, or missionaries in general, and for our government. The prayer of intercession should generally not last more than 10-15 minutes.

It's also good practice to engage in a brief time of prayer just before the sermon and after the sermon. I usually then offer a final benediction/prayer at the very end of the entire worship service.[47] There will be some who will complain about the amount of time spent in prayer, but I agree with Mark Dever who said "we should pray so much in our church gatherings that the nonbelievers get bored. We talk too much to a God they don't believe in."[48]

Public Reading of God's Word. In 1 Timothy 4:13 Paul commands Timothy, "Until I come, devote yourself to the public reading of Scripture." The church in Ephesus was a mixture of Gentile and Jewish believers (Eph. 2:11-22). Paul most likely gave this command because in the New Testament church not everyone had access to God's word; thus, it was important for God's word to be read to them on Sunday. They needed to be made familiar with the Old Testament stories, God's commands, and how Jesus Christ was the fulfillment of the entire Old Testament. Most of us today have easy access to God's word and can read it whenever we choose. For this reason, many think there is no need for so much Bible reading during corporate worship. Churches *really* only need to read the sermon passage. However, according to one survey conducted in 2020, 55% of professing Christians said they read their Bibles three to four times or less per year. Hence, it still makes sense to do much scripture reading during corporate worship for those who might fall into that 55% category. For many Christians, the only place they will ever hear the entire Bible read is in church.

We live in a time when many Christians suffer from Bible illiteracy. They simply are not familiar with their Bibles. Despite the fact that "all Scripture is breathed out by God and profitable for teaching, for reproof, for correction, and for

---

[47] See Appendixes A for a sample of an ideal church liturgy.
[48] Mark Dever, cited in John Onwuchekwa, *Prayer: How Praying Together Shapes the Church* (Wheaton, IL: Crossway, 2018), 15.

training in righteousness, that the man of God may be complete, equipped for every good work" (2 Tim. 3:16-17), many Christians don't read it daily, and those who do, do not read it consecutively but jump around, here and there, never really grasping the full story of redemptive history. There are probably some in your congregation who are not reading their Bible daily or consecutively; thus, we should want to do all that we can to give them a heavy dose on Sunday. We should want our people to be saturated with God's word. For this reason, it is wise to do several different readings during the Sunday corporate worship service.

At the beginning of the service there should be a *Call to Worship* where a portion of scripture is read which beckons the people to come and worship their King (e.g., 1 Chron. 16:8-10; Ps. 19:1-6; Is. 6:1-7). The worship should also include the *Reading of the Law*, a portion of scripture from either the Old or New Testament which communicates God's demands upon his people (e.g., Ex. 20:1-11; Matt. 5:27-30; Rom. 12:9-13). Though we are no longer under law, but under grace, God still requires his people to live by a certain set of standards, to pursue "holiness without which no one will see the Lord" (Rom. 6:14; Heb. 12:14).

Immediately after the *Reading of the Law* is where we engage in our *Prayer of Confession* (see above). This is then followed by a portion of scripture reading we call the *Assurance of Pardon*. As the title implies, this is a portion of scripture which reminds the people that, despite their sin and failures, with God there is an abundance of grace and forgiveness (e.g., Ps. 103:11-14; 1 John 1:9). When we've been through a tough week, when we've struggled with sin, it is good to be reminded of the gospel, to be reminded that because of our union with Christ through faith, God remembers our sins no more (Jer. 31:34).

At this point in the liturgy, our congregation stands and reads together either the Lord's Prayer or a portion of a historic creed. We typically circulate between the Apostle's Creed, the Nicene Creed, the Chalcedonian Creed, and the Athanasian Creed. Though there is no expressed command in scripture to publicly read historic confessions as part of the Lord's Day worship, elders are exhorted to teach the "whole counsel of God," to "give instruction in sound doctrine," and to faithfully "hold to the traditions" as they have been passed down to us (Acts 20:27; Titus 1:9; 2 Thess. 2:15). Reading historic confessions during the Lord's Day worship service is a great way to do this and to expose the congregation to wonderful, historic, and biblical truths. The reading schedule our church follows takes us through seventeen weeks, and then we start over. This is a long enough period of time that the congregation does not feel this is mundane, but it is also a short enough timeframe for us to read through each confession three times per year.[49]

The Preaching of God's Word. Paul says to young Timothy whom he has left in Ephesus to pastor the church there, "I charge you in the presence of God and of Christ Jesus, who is to judge the living and the dead, and by his appearing and his kingdom: preach the word; be ready in season and out of season; reprove, rebuke, and exhort, with complete patience and teaching" (2 Tim. 4:1-2). Paul uses strong language by essentially placing Timothy under oath—"I charge you in the presence of God..." The Reformers understood the importance and centrality of the preaching of God's word, which is why many of them moved

---

[49] See Appendix B for a list of confessional readings throughout the year.

the pulpit from the side of the sanctuary to the center. This was not to highlight the importance of the preacher, but the importance of God's word proclaimed.

Many churches make the mistake of downplaying the importance of preaching and instead emphasize the importance of the worship music, small group Bible studies, discipleship, outreach ministries, so on and so forth. This is often evident from the short fifteen-minute homily and forty minutes of singing. This is not to say that other areas of ministry are not important. They certainly are. But Paul solemnly charged Timothy to "preach the word" and in so doing to "reprove, rebuke, and exhort, with complete patience and teaching." He tells him he must do this because there will come a time "when people will not endure sound teaching, but having itching ears they will accumulate for themselves teachers to suit their own passions, and will turn away from listening to the truth and wander off into myths" (vv.3-4). Regarding 2 Timothy 4:1-2, Wilson states that "the preaching of the word is the point at which doctrine intersects with our lives, at which reproof confronts our lives, at which correction corrects. And of course, the point is not that when the Bible is read it *cannot* do this…But the point is that the ordinary means which God has chosen for the transformation of the world is *the preached word*. And when the word of God is faithfully preached, Christ is preaching."[50]

However, it is not just the preaching of God's word that matters but the *expository* preaching of God's word. In Acts 20 when Paul is offering some final instructions to the elders of the church in Ephesus, he exhorts them to follow his example and reminds them how he "did not shrink from declaring to you the

---

[50] Wilson, *Mother Kirk*, 69.

whole counsel of God" (v.27). The only way a minister can be certain of declaring to the church "the whole counsel of God" and not inadvertently skipping over the difficult or uncomfortable texts is through verse-by-verse expository/exegetical preaching. Certainly, there is a time and a place for topical series in order to hone the church's understanding of a specific subject. Nevertheless, the sheep will be healthier and receive a more balanced diet when preachers walk through books of the Bible.

The primary way most Christians will learn how to handle and study their Bibles is by observing the man behind the pulpit. Few Christians will ever read a book on hermeneutics or sit through a class or small group study on how to study the Bible. Most who attend church every week will learn how to properly handle, rightly interpret, and correctly understand a passage of scripture in light of its literary and historical context by watching how the preacher handles the text. Is he taking a passage of scripture and reading something into it that no one else could possibly see was there or is he asking questions like, 'What was the original intended message by the original author to the original audience?' 'How would the original audience have understood this passage and applied it to their own lives?' Expositional preaching makes for healthy Christians which makes for healthy churches.

Singing of Psalms, Hymns, and Spiritual Songs. To the church in Ephesus, the same church Timothy is pastoring, Paul commands that they are to encourage "one another in psalms and hymns and spiritual songs" (Eph. 5:19). We see Paul commanding the church in Colossae to do the same. "Let the word of Christ dwell in you richly, teaching and admonishing one another in all wisdom, singing psalms and hymns and spiritual songs, with thankfulness in your hearts to God" (Col. 3:16). While there is not universal agreement as to the meaning of "psalms and hymns and spiritual songs", there is agreement that these words are not synonymous. The first century use of the Greek words (*psalmos*, *humnos*, and *ode*), Charles Hodge explains, "appears to have been as loose as that of the corresponding English terms, *psalm*, *hymn*, *song*, is with us. A psalm was a hymn, and a hymn a song. Still there was a distinction between them as there is still."[51] Thus, these terms would appear to reference different categories of music/songs. Hence, the worship wars that go on in many of our churches are superfluous at best and unbiblical at worst.

The point is that scripture commands there be singing in corporate worship, and there seems to be no limit as to the kind of instruments that may be used (Psalm 150). That God commands singing with instruments is the first and most obvious reason to do so. However, a second obvious reason is that God simply desires and enjoys it. There must be a reason the Psalter is the largest book in the Bible. The book of Psalm was the worship book of God's people. We read these psalms and refer to them as Hebrew poetry, which they certainly are, but these psalms were sung by the people of God and were used for corporate worship. The book of Psalm communicates to us, among other things, that God loves to be worshiped, exalted, and sung to.

For this reason, worship should be primarily directed heavenward. Kauflin is correct when he states, "Worship in the wrong direction is called idolatry. It's looking to anything other

---

[51] Charles Hodge, *Commentary on the Epistle to the Ephesians* (Grand Rapids, MI: William B. Eerdmans Publishing Co., reprinted 1994), 303-304.

than God for our ultimate satisfaction, comfort, security, or joy."[52] The songs we sing in corporate worship should be biblically sound and theologically accurate. Our theology is shaped as much by what we sing in church as by what is read and preached from across the pulpit. Hence, the apostle's admonishment that we are to be "teaching and admonishing one another in all wisdom, singing psalms and hymns and spiritual songs." As we engage in biblical worship that is God-glorifying, Christ-exalting, and biblically sound, we not only bring glory to God by extolling the magnificence of his person and the riches of his grace and mercy, but we also edify the saints and fortify their faith by teaching and encouraging one another through song.

In the end, the Church exists for the worship of God; thus, when we come to church, we come there primarily to worship God and to exalt his Son through the various aspects of the worship service. Everything done in corporate worship should ultimately exalt the glory of the resurrected Christ.

Collection of Tithes and Offerings. In the Old Testament, the people of God were to give tithes and offerings to the Levites "for their service that they do, their service in the tent of meeting" (Num. 18:21-24). They were to do this out of obedience to what God commands, but also as a form of worship. This is seen in Deuteronomy 12 where God commands the people not to worship him in the same manner that the surrounding nations worship their gods. He says to them, "You shall not worship the LORD your God in that way. But you shall seek the place that the LORD your God will choose out of all your tribes to put his name and make his habitation there. There

---

[52] Bob Kauflin, *True Worshippers: Seeking What Matters to God* (Wheaton, IL: Crossway, 2015), 50.

you shall go, and there you shall bring your burnt offerings and your sacrifices, *your tithes and the contribution that you present*, your vow offerings, your freewill offerings, and the firstborn of your herd and of your flock" (vv.4-6, emphasis added). Thus, as a means of worship, the people were to bring their offerings to the designated meeting place between God and his people, the place where God would "put his name and make his habitation"—*the temple in Jerusalem*.

In the New Testament we see similar commands being given to the church. Like the Levites of the Old Testament, we see the church being commanded to provide for those who "labor in preaching and teaching" (1 Tim. 5:17-18) and to "share all good things with the one who teaches" (Gal. 6:6; cf. Rom. 15:27; 1 Cor. 9:8-11). We also see Paul directing the church in Corinth to take up a collection "on the first day of every week"—the Lord's Day (1 Cor. 16:1-4). Thus, the collection of tithes and offerings is something that ought to be done every Lord's Day as a part of the corporate worship service—as a means of worship.

The giving of tithes and offerings is itself a form of worship, and the amount one gives reflects the degree of worth one ascribes to God. While in the Old Testament God commanded that the people give a tenth of all that God had given to them, we see no such command in the New Testament. Instead, what we see in the New Testament (2 Cor. 8-9) is that when Paul seeks to encourage the church in Corinth to be cheerful givers, he points them to the cross of Christ and reminds them about "the grace of our Lord Jesus Christ, that though he was rich, yet for your sake he became poor, so that you by his poverty might become rich" (8:9). In other words, Paul is essentially saying that if you want to know how much of your income to give back to God, look to the cross of Christ and ask yourself how much is that worth? Sadly, however, according to a recent survey, 68% of professing evangelicals give less than 2% of their income in tithes and offerings. For most evangelicals, Christ's atoning sacrifice on the cross for their sins is worth less than two cents on the dollar.[53]

The Sacrament of the Lord's Supper. It is clear from scripture that the New Testament church made a practice of participating in the sacrament of the Lord's Supper on the first day of every week (Acts 2:42; 20:7; 1 Cor. 11:18, 20, 23-26). The "breaking of bread" is the first century phrase for partaking in the Lord's Supper, and we know that the church gathered on the first day of every week for worship and for the taking up of offerings (Acts 20:7; 1 Cor. 16:2). Thus, while there is no explicit command to partake of the Lord's Supper every Sunday, it seems unwise to break with the tradition of the New Testament church.

A very likely reason they practiced the Lord's Supper every week was because of their biblical understanding of the meaning and spiritual value of the sacrament. What is happening in the Lord's Supper and why do we do it? Following is a brief survey of the various views of the Lord's Supper, culminating in what I believe to be a biblical view of the sacrament.[54]

Transubstantiation. This is the view held by the Roman Catholic Church which states that a miracle takes place in the words of institution when the Lord's Supper is given, that the

---

[53] Grey Matter Research and Infinity Concepts, "The Tithing Tenth" in *Christianity Today* (January/February 2022).
[54] The survey of the various views of the Lord's Supper has been adopted from a sermon titled "Supping with Christ: Christ's Presence and the Lord's Supper" delivered by Hexon Maldonado on July 5, 2020.

bread and wine are literally and actually changed into the body and blood of Christ. The elements may look, feel, and taste like bread and wine, but they are the actual flesh and blood of Christ. The *substance of the elements* is transformed; hence the name, *trans-substance,* or Transubstantiation.

Roman Catholicism argues this based on Jesus' words, "This is my body." They argue that "This is my body" must mean "*This is my actual body*." Jesus also said, "This is my blood". Thus, in some sense it must be the *actual body and blood* of Christ. Furthermore, Jesus seems to lay the groundwork for the transubstantial understanding of the Lord's Supper in John 6:32-57. However, one must keep in mind that Jesus is talking about himself as *that which came down from heaven to give life*, and that by believing is how one gains eternal life. Jesus is not saying we must literally eat his flesh or drink his blood to have eternal life, rather he is describing the degree of faith we must have in Christ for eternal life. Just as the Israelites in the wilderness were wholly dependent on the manna from heaven to live, so also believers must be wholly dependent on Christ to live. Just as the Israelites in the wilderness could not save any of the manna for the next day but had to consume it all, so also by faith we must take in all of Christ. We must embrace all his person and work and teachings to have eternal life. We cannot be lukewarm when it comes to faith in Christ.

The Roman Church also argues from 1 Corinthians 10:16 that we are eating and drinking Christ's flesh and blood. However, whatever v.16 means, it must carry the same meaning as in v.18. "Consider the people of Israel: are not those who eat the sacrifices *participants in the altar?*" Those who ate the sacrifice did not in some way eat the altar. Rather, Israelites who ate the sacrifice in some sense became connected to the altar itself. So also, one cannot eat the elements of the Lord's Supper without in some sense being connected to the body and blood of Christ, the person of Christ. Thus, Roman Catholicism carries the language of Christ too far and places more weight upon the text than it can bear.

Consubstantiation. Transubstantiation was the dominant view of the church for approximately five-hundred years until the time of reformation when Martin Luther, a German monk, argued for a spiritual presence of Christ in the Lord's Supper. Luther ends up moving away from Rome's view of the Lord's Supper, but more for theological reasons rather than exegetical reasons. It's not so much that he had a problem with the way the Roman Church interpreted the texts of scripture, but he strongly disagreed with the theology which lay behind the Catholic understanding of the Lord's Supper.

By the time of the Reformation, the early 1500's, Rome had come to believe that not only are we consuming the actual body and blood of Christ in the Lord's Supper, but that the elements were a means of earning infused righteousness from Christ. The Lord's Supper had come to be one of the seven sacraments of the church through which we earn righteousness from God. Luther, of course, came to understand that we do not earn righteousness from God, and we certainly are not infused with righteousness, thereby making us inherently righteous. Rather we are credited with Christ's righteousness which comes to us by faith alone in Christ alone. Thus, Luther rejected Rome's view of the Lord's Supper, understanding that nothing we do can earn righteousness from God.

Nevertheless, Luther was captivated by the words of Christ: "This is my body." In wanting to be faithful to the words of Christ, Luther argued for a more Augustinian view of the Lord's

Supper which came to be known as Consubstantiation. As the words imply: *con* (with) + *substance* = with the substance or with the elements. Luther came to believe that Christ was actually present in and with the elements of the Lord's Supper and we are truly consuming Christ; however, the elements remain unchanged. The bread and wine look, feel, and taste like bread and wine because they *are bread and wine*. However, he maintained that when Jesus said, "This is my body", that must be taken literally. For example, he states:

> For my part, if I cannot fathom how the bread is the body of Christ, yet I will take my reason captive to the obedience of Christ [2 Cor. 10:5], and clinging simply to his words, firmly believe not only that the body of Christ is in the bread, but that the bread is the body of Christ. My warrant for this is the words which say: "He took bread, and when he had given thanks, he broke it and said, 'Take, eat, this (that is, this bread, which he had taken and broken) is my body'" [1 Cor. 11:23-24].[55]

A significant problem with Luther's view; however, is that he was not consistent. In John 10:9 Jesus says, "I am the door", and in John 15:5 he says, "I am the vine; you are the branches." Luther understood that Jesus is not saying he is actually a door or a vine, and we are not actually branches. He rightly understood Jesus to be using metaphorical and symbolic language. While it is admirable for Luther to want to interpret scripture literally, not all scripture is intended to be interpreted literally. For instance, no one interprets the entire book of Revelation literally. Thus, when Christ said, "This is my body",

---

[55] Martin Luther, "The Babylonian Captivity of the Church" in *Martin Luther's Basic Theological Writings*, ed. Timothy F. Lull (Minneapolis, MN: Fortress Press, 1989), 290.

he did not mean we are literally eating his body and drinking his blood.

Symbolism. Ulrich Zwingli, a contemporary of Luther who was leading a reformation of his own in Switzerland, held that transubstantiation and consubstantiation were both wrong. He based this understanding on Jesus's words from John 6 where Christ talks about eating his flesh and drinking his blood. However, he saw v.63 as a key verse in understanding Jesus' words. "It is the Spirit who gives life; *the flesh is no help at all.*" Zwingli argued that salvation is a spiritual matter and is the work of the Holy Spirit. What we do in the flesh makes no difference at all. Zwingli came to understand that Jesus' words "This is my body" and "This is my blood" meant that the bread and wine were symbolic or a picture of Jesus's body and blood. This view has come to be known as the Zwinglian or the symbolic view of the Lord's Supper.

The greatest flaw with this view is the strong warning given in 1 Corinthians 11:27-30 against partaking of the Lord's Supper in an unworthy manner. There is no such warning attached to baptism which all evangelicals agree is symbolic. Baptism is a symbolic picture of having died with Christ and then being resurrected to walk in newness of life. Baptism is not meritorious. Hence, nowhere does the Bible warn that if an unbeliever is inadvertently baptized, God's wrath will come upon the baptized or the baptizer. That there is a strong warning attached to inappropriate use of the Lord's Supper, and not to baptism, means that the Lord's Supper must be more than symbolic, but less than transubstantiation or consubstantiation.

Reformed View. Others, such as John Calvin, held that Christ is and remains in bodily form, seated at the right hand of God the Father and, therefore, cannot be *physically present* in or with the elements. Nevertheless, when Paul writes "The cup of blessing that we bless, is it not a participation in the blood of Christ? The bread that we break, is it not a participation in the body of Christ?" (1 Cor. 10:16), he must mean that in some way and in some sense, we do participate in the body and blood of Christ.

This explains the strong warning for those who partake of the sacrament in an unworthy manner. Calvin understood that in a *spiritual sense*; that is, *by the power of the Holy Spirit*, Christ is present in and with the elements, though not bodily or physically. Thus, because it is spiritual, we are not *actually* eating Christ's flesh and blood. Christ does not descend from heaven and enter the elements for our consumption. Nevertheless, his presence in and with the elements—by means of the Holy Spirit—is as real as the Holy Spirit is real, as real as God is real. Though we cannot see God, we understand that God is real and present with us in corporate worship. Thus, in a spiritual, *yet very real sense*, Christ is present in and with the elements. For instance, Calvin states:

> The same body, therefore, which the Son of God once offered to the Father in sacrifice, he daily offers us in the Supper as spiritual food. Only, as I lately hinted, we must hold in regard to the mode, that it is not necessary that the essence of the flesh should descend from heaven in order to our being fed upon it, the virtue of the Spirit being sufficient to break through all the impediments and surmount any distance of place. Meanwhile we deny not that this mode is incomprehensible to the human mind; because neither can flesh naturally be the life of the soul, nor exert its power upon us from heaven, nor without reason is the communion which makes us flesh of the flesh of Christ, and bone of his bones,

called by Paul, "A great mystery." (Eph. V. 30.) Therefore, in the sacred Supper, we acknowledge a miracle which surpasses both the limits of nature and the measure of our sense,...[56]

In the partaking of the sacrament, we are both consuming Christ, *spiritually*, and we are supping with Christ. For this reason, Paul warns in 1 Corinthians 10:21, "You cannot drink the cup of the Lord and the cup of demons. You cannot partake of the table of the Lord and the table of demons. Shall we provoke the Lord to jealousy?" In other words, do not think you can live any way you want, out there in the world, and then come into the King's throne room on Sunday morning and sit at his table and partake of his supper without incurring his wrath.

This truth will lead Paul to issue his strong warning against unbelievers, or believers living in unrepentant sin, partaking of the Lord's Supper. For an unbeliever, or a believer living in active unrepentant sin, to attempt to sit at the table of the Lord and participate in the Lord's Supper is like an Israelite in Exodus 19 attempting to touch the foot of Mt. Sinai before God had entered covenant relationship with the nation of Israel. Only those in covenant relationship with Christ, and only believers who are not actively and intentionally violating the covenant, may enter his presence and sit at his table and participate in the sacrament of the Lord's Supper.

Just as the disciples came together for that first Lord's Supper in the upper room, when we come together for corporate worship and participate in the sacrament of the Lord's Supper, *in a spiritual yet very real sense*, we are consuming Christ and

---

[56] John Calvin, "The Best Method of Obtaining Concord, Provided the Truth be Sought without Contention" in *Tracts and Letters* (IL: Banner of Truth Trust, 2009), 577.

are supping with him at his table. Christ is *spiritually yet truly present* in and with the elements of the Lord's Supper in a more palpable way than at any other time.

When the saints gather for corporate worship on the Lord's Day, minimally the church is to engage in prayer, the reading and preaching of God's word, the singing of psalms, hymns, and spiritual songs, the collection of offerings, and the sacrament of the Lord's Supper. Not only are these the minimal requirements laid out in scripture for the church, but these are also the only activities which should be included in corporate worship. Anything more or less would be to add or subtract from that which God has commanded (Deut. 12:32; 1 Cor. 4:6). Our King has made clear in scripture how he is to be approached and worshiped and "how one ought to behave in the household of God, which is the church of the living God" (1 Tim. 3:15).

Chapter 9
Conclusion

*The fear of the LORD is the beginning of wisdom,
and the knowledge of the Holy One is insight.*
Proverbs 9:10

When the saints gather for corporate worship on the Lord's Day, whether that be in a church building, an auditorium, a gymnasium, a movie theater, or a small clearing in the woods, we would do well to remember that Jesus is King. He is the King of kings and the Lord of lords, and he is *our King*. He is just as much a king and just as real of a king as any king alive on earth today or any king who has lived throughout the history of mankind. To speak of Jesus as king is not the same as calling my daughter a princess or referring to my wife as 'my queen.' Referring to Jesus as King is more than an honorary title or term of endearment. It is the very essence of who he is. He is the King of all creation, the Sovereign of the universe, who sits upon his great throne and rules with a mighty arm and is moving all of world history toward its foreordained conclusion.

As humans who struggle to live by faith and not by sight, we often fail to treat and worship Christ with the reverence and awe he so richly deserves because we cannot see him. And because we cannot see him, because we cannot see his magnificent crown upon his head, because we cannot see the train of his robe filling the temple as Isaiah did, we find it easy to enter his throne room with the same mental attitude as entering a movie theater—casual, drinks and snacks in hand, ready to be entertained. We would never pay a visit to our most favorite

U.S. President or to the monarch of a powerful nation with the same cavalier approach as we do on Sunday mornings.

Many commit the error of thinking that God does not care how we engage in corporate worship, how we approach him, or what we do in worship, as if the God of the Old Testament is not the same as the God of the New Testament. They unwittingly adopt Marcion's view that Jesus is not the God of the Old Testament. But Jesus *is the God of the Old Testament*; thus, he is the same yesterday, today, and forever (Heb. 13:8). How God desires to be approached and worshiped and honored does not change with the coming of Christ. It does not change with the destruction of the temple in AD 70. It does not change with the disappearance of the Levitical priesthood. It does not change merely because God became human and allowed his creatures to gather around him and touch him and know him, face to face. In fact, that God was willing to become a man and take on human flesh and suffer and die for us should cause us to revere and worship and honor him even more.

Christ is the king of the Church, and the visible church is his throne room. The gathering of the saints for corporate worship on the Lord's Day, wherever that might be—a living room, a basement, a rented banquet hall—becomes the throne room of our King. Christians struggle with this because the place where we often gather does not look like a throne room. It looks like an ordinary building. It looks like a basement. It looks like a gymnasium. We understand that God is omnipresent; thus, can it rightly be said that the corporate gathering of the saints for worship is the throne room of Christ? But we walk by faith and not by sight (2 Cor. 5:7). Simply because we cannot see Christ does not mean he is not as real as you and me. Because we cannot see the Holy Spirit does not mean he does not exist. That we cannot see Satan or his demons does not mean we are not engaged in real spiritual battle. That we cannot see God's kingdom advancing does not mean the kingdom is not truly here or that language regarding God's kingdom in scripture is metaphorical. God's kingdom is *real* and is advancing. That the corporate gathering of the saints for worship in a gym, living room, or church building does not look like the inside of Buckingham Palace in no way diminishes the reality that we are standing in the throne room of our King. We are standing in *the King's presence*.

This reality is made all the more clear when we realize that the temple—the household of God—is reconstructed every time the saints gather for corporate worship. Just as the tabernacle in the Old Testament was disassembled each time the pillar of fire moved by night or the pillar of cloud moved by day, and then when it stopped, all the various parts and pieces of furnishing were brought back together to form the tabernacle. Each time that happened, the glory of God would fill the temple (Ex. 40:34-38). Of course, this does not mean God was not present with his people as the tabernacle was being transported. It does, however, mean that the tabernacle was the designated meeting place between God and his people. It was holy ground. It was a mobile Mt. Sinai, a mobile throne room. God was present at that moment in time and in that place in a more palpable way than anywhere else on earth. So also, every believer is a "living stone" of God's temple (1 Peter 2:4-5). When the saints gather for corporate worship, they reconstruct God's temple on earth by means of coming together, and the glory and presence of God is in that place in a more palpable way than any other place on earth. The corporate gathering of the saints for worship—

church—becomes holy ground, the temple of the living God, the throne room of our God and King.

After corporate worship, as the saints go their separate ways and live their lives throughout the week, the tabernacle is disassembled. This does not mean God is not with his people or that they cannot pray to him or worship him throughout the week, but that we should long to come together once again on the Lord's Day to reconstruct the temple of God and enter his most powerful presence, his throne room, and worship at his feet.

Once the tabernacle is reconstructed, like the priests of the Old Testament era, believers minister in his presence, offering "spiritual sacrifices" to God (1 Peter 2:5). All believers are a "royal priesthood" (1 Peter 2:9). We are the priests of God who go about doing the Lord's work within his temple, acting as intermediaries between God and those outside the temple, praying for them and interceding on their behalf. We offer sacrifices of praise and worship to God which rise up to him as a sweet-smelling incense.

Like the Old Testament priests, we are charged with defending and caring for the household of God—the visible church—ensuring that she is not desecrated or used in an unholy manner (1 Cor. 5:1-13). As God's priests, we are called to minister his word to the outside world, being given the ministry of reconciliation and called to be ambassadors for Christ (2 Cor. 5:18-20). The corporate gathering of the saints for worship is God's temple on earth, and we are his priests. There is no greater honor than to be a priest of God, and there is no higher calling than to be called to minister within his temple. What an incredible privilege and honor we have been given to serve as his priests within his throne room and in the presence of our

King. How sad so many believers approach and enter corporate worship with no greater reverence than attending a high school graduation ceremony, some with no greater reverence than attending a bachelor party. As God's priests, he has made clear to us how we should conduct ourselves in his household (1 Tim. 3:15), what things should and should not be done within his temple, and it is our responsibility to ensure the desires of our king are carried out. When the saints gather for corporate worship, we are not to be creative or imaginative. We are not to borrow from the world, looking to see what they do to be successful and attract people to their business. We must not look to see what the fastest growing megachurches are doing and how we can incorporate their tactics into our worship. As God's priests, we are not called to do what makes sense in our mind. We are called to be obedient to his word. Our king has made clear in scripture how he desires to be approached, reverenced, and worshiped. There are ordinarily six activities we are commanded to carry out in corporate worship. Prayer, the reading and proclaiming of God's word, the singing of psalms, hymns, and spiritual songs, the collection of tithes and offerings, and the sacrament of the Lord's Supper (and occasionally baptism). To not carry out these tasks or to go beyond them is to add or subtract from God's word, to deviate from that which God has prescribed, to go beyond what is written (Deut. 12:29-32; 1 Cor 4:6).

For these reasons, we should approach corporate worship on the Lord's Day with a spirit of reverence and awe. We should recognize the gathering of the saints for corporate worship for the magnificent and majestic event it truly is. When we enter the sanctuary, or wherever we gather for worship, that place becomes holy and sacred ground. That place becomes the temple of the God of creation, the throne room of our king, and the glory of the LORD fills that place with his power and presence. For that moment, we cease to exist in this world as we step onto the foreign soil of God's embassy on earth. For that moment, heaven comes down to us as we experience heaven on earth.

It can be easy to think this view is a bit far-fetched, if we do not take scripture at face-value and if we are driven more by our sight than by God's word. Undoubtedly, this was the trouble the Jewish people fell into over time. When the tabernacle was first erected, after all the miracles God had performed to deliver them from Egypt, and after the glory of God filled the tabernacle, it was easy for them to see that this was most definitely the throne room of their king. After Solomon completed the building of the temple with all its shining gold and glitz, and with all the pomp and ceremony, it was easy for them to believe this must be the house of the living God. But as time went on, as people walked past it, as people traveled to it week after week, month after month, year after year, for all the various ceremonies and offerings, it became nothing more than a building, a place where cattle and sheep could be sold. This is what angered Christ (Matt 21:12-17). Regardless of what their senses could or could not perceive, the temple in Jerusalem was still the house of God, the throne room of their king. Like the Jewish people of Jesus' day, for many believers traveling to church week after week, month after month, year after year, corporate worship has become mundane and ordinary. The place where they meet has become nothing more than a conference center, a place to host Trunk-or-Treat parties, Boy Scout meetings, piano recitals, retirement celebrations, church business meetings, and a slew of other events. Thus, it is difficult for them to see corporate worship and the place of corporate worship as anything else. They are driven more by their sense of sight than by what God has told them in his word. In more ways than we realize, many churches have become like those selling sheep and goats in God's sacred home—*even on Sunday morning.*

How then should we prepare for Sunday morning? We should prepare ourselves to enter the King's presence spiritually, mentally, and physically. Spiritually, we dare not approach corporate worship, and especially the Lord's Table, with unconfessed and unrepentant sin in our hearts and lives. Jesus says, "If you are offering your gift at the altar and there remember that your brother has something against you, leave your gift there before the altar and go. First be reconciled to your brother, and then come and offer your gift" (Matt. 5:23-24). In other words, before you engage in the formal act of worship, if you know there is conflict between you and a fellow believer, you should first go and be reconciled to them before you enter corporate worship—the throne room of our king—and offer him your worship. The reason is simple. It is nothing short of hypocrisy to come into God's presence and praise and worship him for his amazing grace and forgiveness when we are unwilling to extend grace and forgiveness toward others. To say, "Jesus, thank you for forgiving me of my sins, but I refuse to forgive my fellow believer for whom you suffered and died" is to make a mockery of God's grace and invite his anger.

It is for this reason Paul warns that whoever partakes of the Lord's Supper "in an unworthy manner will be guilty concerning the body and blood of the Lord." He goes on to exhort that a person must "examine himself, then, and so eat of the bread and drink of the cup" in a worthy manner. The person who does not examine his own heart, search for, and confess unrepentant sin "eats and drinks judgment on himself. That is why many of you are weak and ill, and some have died" (1 Cor. 11:27-30). Hence, leading up to corporate worship, it is imperative to confess to God and turn from any unrepentant sin, and to reconcile broken relationships with other believers.

We should mentally prepare for corporate worship on the Lord's Day by not unnecessarily staying up late the night before. We should desire to come to corporate worship well rested so that we might give our God and King our undivided attention, so that we might be alert and ready to learn, be fed, and hear from him. For parents, it is equally important to get the little ones to bed at a decent hour, so they are not sleeping across the pews, but also so they are not irritable from lack of sleep and thus making it difficult for mommy and daddy to pay attention.

Finally, wake up with enough time to comfortably engage in personal prayer and Bible reading time without being rushed. Quite often, even those who engage in consistent personal devotion time will neglect to spend time in prayer and Bible reading on Sunday morning, thinking they are about to engage in much prayer and Bible learning at church. Instead, they choose to have their alarm go off on Sunday morning, jump out of bed, run around the house half asleep getting themselves and the kids ready, scramble out the door, tumble into church, and struggle to fully engage in worship as their mind and spirit are frazzled from the morning rush. Rather, we should spend time on our knees in prayer and Bible reading on the Lord's Day morning, mentally and spiritually preparing ourselves for the magnificent event in which we are about to engage.

We should physically prepare for corporate worship by getting things ready the night before. This prevents us from running around rushed on Sunday morning, feeling frazzled and frustrated when we cannot find the children's shoes or, worse, we cannot find our own shoes. We should take the time on Saturday evening to select and press our best attire and lay them out or hang them somewhere so that no thought is needed in the morning to know what to wear. Bibles, notepads, writing instruments, and whatever else that will be taken to church should be gathered the night before and set near the door so that time is not spent looking for these things in the morning.

In short, if we understand what is happening on Sunday morning during corporate worship, if we truly appreciate the magnitude of this momentous occasion, then we should approach corporate worship as though it is one of the most important, if not *the most important*, event in our lives. When we gather with the saints for corporate worship on the Lord's Day, we are entering into the very throne room of our God and King. We are standing in his presence before his throne. Just as in the Old Testament, regarding the tabernacle, God says to the people of Israel that it is there in that place and in that moment that "I will meet with you, and from above the mercy seat, from between the two cherubim that are on the ark of the testimony, I will speak with you" (Ex. 25:22). The Israelites understood that God is omnipresent, that God could speak to them from anywhere and that they could pray to God and worship him anywhere. But they also understood that the tabernacle/temple was the throne room of God, the designated meeting place between the King and his people. So also, the corporate gathering of the saints on the Lord's Day, the New Testament temple, becomes a piece of heaven on earth, God's embassy, the throne room of our God and King, and should be approached and entered accordingly.

God desires that we worship him not just in accordance with scripture, but that we worship him and enter his presence with reverence and awe. This is what the religious leaders of Jesus' day failed to understand. Of them Jesus said, "This people honors me with their lips, but their heart is far from me; in vain do they worship me" (Matt. 15:8-9). The Pharisees and scribes were known for paying meticulous attention to the Law, tithing mint and dill and cumin and yet they still turned the temple courtyard into a marketplace (Matt. 21:12-13; 23:23). To be clear, the Law did not explicitly forbid the selling of sheep and oxen and pigeons within the temple courtyard, but if they understood the sacredness of that place, God should not have had to tell them not to bring animals into his throne room. They took the approach that since God had not specifically forbidden the selling of animals in the temple courtyard (*normative principle*), then he must not care. Today our churches are filled with modern-day Pharisees who intellectually recognize that the corporate gathering of the saints on the Lord's Day is holy ground, is the very throne room of our God and King, is heaven brought down to earth, is God's embassy, is the designated meeting place between God and his people, and that we stand in the very presence of the living God, but since scripture does not explicitly command how we should present ourselves before the King in corporate worship and how we should engage in corporate worship, *God must not care*. But God should not have to tell us how we should enter his presence. If we have a biblical understanding of corporate worship and a reverence for God, how we enter the throne room of Christ should be obvious. "The fear of the LORD is the beginning of wisdom, and the knowledge of the Holy One is insight" (Prov. 9:10).

Appendix A
Sample Liturgy for Corporate Worship

Prayer of Invocation	
Call to Worship	Psalm 24:7-10
Song of Entrance	"O Worship the King"
Reading of the Law	Deuteronomy 6:4-9
Prayer of Confession	
Assurance of Pardon	1 John 1:9
Prayer of Intercession	
Confessional Reading	Apostles' Creed (ca. 2nd century)
Songs of Praise	"When I Survey"
	"O for a Thousand Tongues"
Reading of Sermon Passage	
Prayer of Illumination	
Message from God's Word	*Beholding the Glory of Christ*
Prayer of Supplication	
Sacrament of the Lord's Supper	
Doxology or Gloria Patri	
Departing Song	"Amazing Grace"
Benediction	Numbers 6:24-26

Appendix B
Confessional Readings for Corporate Worship

Below are sixteen readings from historic confessions, plus the Lord's Prayer, for a total of seventeen readings, which can be used during the Sunday morning worship service. One section is read each Lord's Day for seventeen weeks, the cycle then begins over again. Seventeen weeks is a long enough time so that the congregation does not feel we are reading these too often, but short enough to go through them three times per year. In our church, the congregation stands and reads these in unison.

Apostles' Creed (ca. 2nd century)
1. I believe in God the Father Almighty, maker of heaven and earth; And in Jesus Christ, his only begotten Son, our Lord, who was conceived by the Holy Spirit, born of the Virgin Mary, suffered under Pontius Pilate, was crucified, dead, and was buried; He descended into hell. On the third day he rose again from the dead; he ascended into heaven, is seated at the right hand of the Father, and will come again to judge the living and the dead. I believe in the Holy Spirit, the [one] holy…church, the communion of saints, the forgiveness of sins, the resurrection of the body and the life everlasting. Amen.

The Nicene Creed (AD 325/381)
2. I believe in one God, the Father Almighty, Maker of heaven and earth, and of all things visible and invisible. And in one Lord Jesus Christ, the only-begotten Son of God, begotten of the Father before all worlds; God of God, Light of Light, very God of very God; begotten, not

    made, being of one substance with the Father, by whom all things were made.
3. [Christ], for us men and for our salvation, came down from heaven and was incarnate by the Holy Spirit of the Virgin Mary, and was made man; and was crucified also for us under Pontius Pilate; he suffered and was buried; and the third day he rose again, according to the Scriptures; and ascended into heaven, and sits on the right hand of the Father; and he shall come again, with glory, to judge the living and the dead; whose kingdom shall have no end.
4. And I believe in the Holy Spirit, the Lord and Giver of life; who proceeds from the Father and the Son; who with the Father and the Son together is worshiped and glorified; who spoke by the prophets. And I believe in one holy [universal] and apostolic church. I acknowledge one baptism for the remission of sins; and I look for the resurrection of the dead, and the life of the world to come. Amen.

Chalcedonian Creed (AD 451)
5. Therefore, following the holy fathers, we all unite in teaching that we should confess one and the same Son, our Lord Jesus Christ. This same one is perfect in deity, and the same one is perfect in humanity; the same one is true God and true man, comprising a rational soul and a body.
6. [Christ] is of the same essence as the Father according to his deity, and the same one is of the same essence with us according to his humanity, like us in all things except sin. He was begotten before the ages from the Father according to his deity, but in the last days for us and our

salvation, the same one was born of the Virgin Mary, the bearer of God, according to his humanity.

7. He is one and the same Christ, Son, Lord, and Only Begotten, who is made known in two natures united unconfusedly, unchangeably, indivisibly, inseparably. The distinction between the natures is not at all destroyed because of the union, but rather the property of each nature is preserved and concurs together into one person and subsistence.

8. He is not separated or divided into two persons, but he is one and the same Son, the Only Begotten, God the Logos, the Lord Jesus Christ. This is the way the prophets spoke of him from the beginning, and Jesus Christ himself instructed us, and the Council of the fathers has handed the faith down to us.

Athanasian Creed (5th century AD)

9. Whoever desires to be saved should above all hold the [Christian] faith. Anyone who does not keep it whole and unbroken will doubtless perish eternally. Now this is the [Christian] faith: That we worship one God in Trinity and the Trinity in unity, neither confounding their persons nor dividing the essence. For the person of the Father is a distinct person, the person of the Son is another, and that of the Holy Spirit still another. But the divinity of the Father, Son, and Holy Spirit is one, the glory equal, the majesty coeternal.

10. Such as the Father is, such is the Son and such is the Holy Spirit. The Father is uncreated, the Son is uncreated, the Holy Spirit is uncreated. The Father is immeasurable, the Son is immeasurable, the Holy Spirit is immeasurable. The Father is eternal, the Son is eternal, the Holy Spirit

is eternal. And yet there are not three eternal beings; there is but one eternal being. So too there are not three uncreated or immeasurable beings; there is but one uncreated and immeasurable being.

11. Similarly, the Father is almighty, the Son is almighty, the Holy Spirit is almighty. Yet there are not three almighty beings; there is but one almighty being. Thus, the Father is God, the Son is God, the Holy Spirit is God. Yet there are not three gods; there is but one God. Thus, the Father is Lord, the Son is Lord, the Holy Spirit is Lord. Yet there are not three lords; there is but one Lord.

12. Just as Christian truth compels us to confess each person individually as both God and Lord, so [Christian] religion forbids us to say that there are three gods or lords. The Father was neither made nor created nor begotten from anyone. The Son was neither made nor created; he was begotten from the Father alone. The Holy Spirit was neither made nor created nor begotten; he proceeds from the Father and the Son. Accordingly, there is one Father, not three fathers; there is one Son, not three sons; there is one Holy Spirit, not three holy spirits.

13. None in this Trinity is before or after, none is greater or smaller; in their entirety the three persons are co-eternal and co-equal with each other. So in everything, as was said earlier, the unity in Trinity, and the Trinity in unity, is to be worshiped. Anyone then who desires to be saved should think thus about the Trinity. But it is necessary for eternal salvation that one also believe in the incarnation of our Lord Jesus Christ faithfully.

14. Now this is the true faith: That we believe and confess that our Lord Jesus Christ, God's Son, is both God and

man, equally. He is God from the essence of the Father, begotten before time; and he is man from the essence of his mother, born in time; completely God, completely man, with a rational soul and human flesh; equal to the Father as regards divinity, less than the Father as regards humanity.

15. Although he is God and man, yet Christ is not two, but one. He is one, however, not by his divinity being turned into flesh, but by God's taking humanity to himself. He is one, certainly not by the blending of his essence, but by the unity of his person. For just as one man is both rational soul and flesh, so too the one Christ is both God and man.

16. He suffered for our salvation; he descended to hell; he arose from the dead on the third day; he ascended to heaven; he is seated at the Father's right hand; from there he will come to judge the living and the dead. At his coming all people will arise bodily and give an accounting of their own deeds. Those who have done good will enter eternal life, and those who have done evil will enter eternal fire. This is the [Christian] faith: That one cannot be saved without believing it firmly and faithfully.

The Lord's Prayer

17. Our Father, who art in heaven, hallowed be thy name; thy kingdom come; thy will be done, on earth as it is in heaven. Give us this day our daily bread. And forgive us our debts as we forgive our debtors. Lead us not into temptation but deliver us from evil. For thine is the kingdom, and the power, and the glory, forever and ever. Amen.

Appendix C
Scripture Readings for Corporate Worship

Call to Worship
Revelation 4:6b-8
Psalm 113:1-4
Revelation 4:8-11
Revelation 5:11-13
Revelation 15:3-4
Psalm 24:7-10
Psalm 33:1-4
Hebrews 12:26-29
Psalm 100
Psalm 66:1-5
Psalm 57:7-11
Isaiah 6:1-3
Psalm 96:1-4
Psalm 118:22-26
Psalm 95:1-6
Psalm 99:1-5
Psalm 117:1-2

Reading of the Law
1 Thessalonians 4:9-12
Hebrews 13:1-5
James 1:19-21
James 1:26-27
James 2:1-4
James 2:8-11
James 2:14-17
James 3:7-10
James 4:1-4
James 4:6b-10
James 4:11-12
1 Peter 1:14-16
1 Peter 2:1-3
1 Peter 2:13-17
1 Peter 3:1-7
1 Peter 3:8-12
1 John 3:11-15
1 John 3:16-18
Ephesians 5:15-21
Ephesians 5:22-33
Ephesians 6:1-4
Ephesians 6:5-9
Matthew 5:2-10
Matthew 6:1-4
Matthew 6:5-8
Matthew 6:16-18
Matthew 6:19-24
Matthew 7:1-5
Matthew 7:12
Matthew 22:34-40
Colossians 3:18-21
Colossians 3:22-4:1
Exodus 20:1-11
Exodus 20:12-17
Matthew 5:21-24
Matthew 5:27-30
Matthew 5:31-32
Matthew 5:33-37
Matthew 5:38-42
Matthew 5:43-48
Matthew 22:34-40
John 15:9-12
Romans 12:9-13
Romans 12:14-18
Romans 12:19-21
Romans 13:1-4a

Romans 13:8-10
1 Corinthians 13:1-7
Ephesians 4:1-3
Ephesians 4:25-28
Ephesians 4:29-32
Colossians 3:5-8
Colossians 3:12-14
Colossians 3:18-21
Colossians 3:22-4:1
Ephesians 5:1-2
Ephesians 5:3-5
Deuteronomy 5:6-11
Deuteronomy 5:12-15
Deuteronomy 5:16-21
Deuteronomy 6:4-9
1 Thessalonians 4:3-8

Romans 5:1-2
Romans 5:6-9
Romans 8:1-2
Romans 8:31-34
Acts 13:36-39
1 Corinthians 15:3-5
2 Corinthians 5:21
Colossians 1:13-14
Galatians 3:11-13
Colossians 2:13-14
Hebrews 4:14-16
Hebrews 7:23-25
Hebrews 10:15-17
1 John 1:8-9
1 John 2:1-2

Assurance of Pardon
Psalm 32:1-5
Psalm 65:1-3
Psalm 86:3-5
Psalm 103:1-5
Psalm 103:11-14
Psalm 130:1-4
Isaiah 1:18
Isaiah 43:24-25
Isaiah 44:22
Isaiah 53:4-6
Isaiah 55:6-7
Jeremiah 31:33-34
Joel 2:12-13
Micah 7:18-19
Matthew 11:28-30
John 3:16
Romans 4:4-8

Works Cited

Beale, Greg. "A Redemptive-Historical Perspective on the Temple." *Biblical Training*, accessed December 3, 2021, https://www.biblicaltraining.org/lecture/135848.

Beeke, Joel R. and Mark Jones. *A Puritan Theology: Doctrine for Life*. Grand Rapids, MI: Reformation Heritage Books, 2012.

Calvin, John. "The Best Method of Obtaining Concord, Provided the Truth be Sought without Contention." *Tracts and Letters*. IL: Banner of Truth Trust, 2009.

Case, Andrew. "Towards a Better Understanding of God's Holiness: Challenging the Status Quo." *The Bible Translator*, no. 68 (2017): 269-283.

Dickie, Robert L. *What the Bible Teaches About Worship*. England: Evangelical Press, 2007.

Gentry, Peter J. "No One *Holy* Like the Lord." *Midwestern Journal of Theology*, no. 12.1 (2013): 17-38.

Gentry, Peter J. and Stephen J. Wellum. *Kingdom through Covenants: A Biblical-Theological Understanding of the Covenants*. Wheaton, IL: Crossway, 2012.

Grey Matter Research and Infinity Concepts. "The Tithing Tenth." *Christianity Today* (January/February 2022).

Hodge, Charles. *Commentary on the Epistle to the Ephesians*. Grand Rapids, MI: William B. Eerdmans Publishing Co., reprinted 1994.

Horton, Michael. *A Better Way: Rediscovering the Drama of Christ-Centered Worship*. Grand Rapids, MI: Baker Books, 2002.

Hughes, P.E. "Priesthood." *Evangelical Dictionary of*

Theology, 2nd ed. Grand Rapids, MI: Baker Book House Company, 2001.

Jones, Jeffrey M. "U.S. Church Membership Falls Below Majority for First Time." Gallup. March 29, 2021, accessed December 29, 2021, https://news.gallup.com/poll/341963/church-membership-falls-below-majority-first-time.aspx.

Kaiser, Walter C., Jr. "Exodus", vol. 2 of *The Expositor's Bible Commentary with the New International Version of the Holy Bible*. Grand Rapids, MI: Zondervan Pub. House, 1990.

Kauflin, Bob. *True Worshippers: Seeking What Matters to God*. Wheaton, IL: Crossway, 2015.

Keil, C.F. and F. Delitzsch, *Commentary on the Old Testament*. Peabody, MA: Hendrickson Publishers, 1866-91; reprint, 2006.

Kelley, Joe Wayne. "Seated in the Heavenlies: Integrating John Calvin's Principles of Worship in a Baptist Context." DMin. diss., Reformed Theological Seminary, 2010.

Luther, Martin. "The Babylonian Captivity of the Church." *Martin Luther's Basic Theological Writings*, ed. Timothy F. Lull. Minneapolis, MN: Fortress Press, 1989.

McCready, W.O. "Priests and Levites." *The International Standard Bible Encyclopedia*. Vol. 3. Grand Rapids, MI: William B. Eerdmans Publishing Company, 1986.

Muis, Jan. "God Our King." *HTS Theological Studies* (2008), accessed December 3, 2021. https://www.academia.edu/50923215/ God_our_King.

Onwuchekwa, John. *Prayer: How Praying Together Shapes the Church*. Wheaton, IL: Crossway, 2018.

Payne, D.F. "King; Kingdom." *The International Standard*

Bible Encyclopedia. Vol. 3. Grand Rapids, MI: William B. Eerdmans Publishing Company, 1986.

Piper, John. *A Baptist Catechism* (revised), www.desiringgod.org.

Sproul, R.C. 1985. *The Holiness of God*. Wheaton, IL: Tyndale House Publishers.

_____. 2013. *How Shall We then Worship: Biblical Principles to Guide Us Today*. Colorado Spring, CO: David C. Cook.

The Book of Church Order of the Presbyterian Church in America. Published by The Office of the Stated Clerk of the General Assembly of the Presbyterian Church in America (2007).

"The Church: Pillar and Ground of the Truth." *The Church Bible Study Set*. New Albany, MS: Mediagratiae, 2021.

The Westminster Confession of Faith (1646).

"What Powers Does Queen Elizabeth II Have?," *The Week*. December 10, 2019, accessed December 3, 2021. https://www.theweek.co.uk/royal-family/97645/how-much-power-does-the-royal-family-have.

Wilson, Douglas. *Mother Kirk: Essays and Forays in Practical Ecclesiology*. Moscow, ID: Canon Press, 2001.

www.ingramcontent.com/pod-product-compliance
Lightning Source LLC
Chambersburg PA
CBHW061647040426
42446CB00010B/1618